Captivating Combinations

Color and Style in the Garden

Norman Winter

UNIVERSITY PRESS OF MISSISSIPPI   JACKSON

Complement—something that completes or makes perfect.

This book is dedicated to Jan, my wife and complement,

who enthusiastically encourages and supports me.

www.upress.state.ms.us
The University Press of Mississippi is a member
of the Association of American University Presses.

Copyright © 2009 by Norman Winter
All rights reserved
Manufactured in Singapore

First printing 2009

All photographs courtesy of Norman Winter, except photographs on the following pages: 000 and 000, courtesy of Terry Howe, Ball Horticultural Co.; 000 and 000,
courtesy of Blooms of Bressingham; 000 and 000, courtesy of the Perennial Plant
Association

Library of Congress Cataloging-in-Publication Data
Winter, Norman.
Captivating combinations : color and style in the garden / Norman Winter.
    p. cm.
Includes bibliographical references and index.
ISBN 978-1-934110-92-8 (cloth : alk. paper) — ISBN 978-1-934110-93-5 (pbk. : alk.
paper) 1. Color in gardening—United States. 2. Plants, Ornamental—Color—United
States. 3. Landscape design—United States. 4. Gardens—United States. I. Title.
SB454.3.C64W57 2009
635.9′68—dc22   2008030397

British Library Cataloging-in-Publication Data available

Contents

Combination Basics

Few things affect the overall look of a garden as much as color. Used effectively, color can create a feeling of calm, graciousness, spaciousness, excitement, or just about any mood we want to achieve. But the effective use of color takes some thought. Some gardeners shop like kids in a candy store—it all looks so enticing that they want a little of everything. Other shoppers are filled with trepidation when visiting the garden center because they simply don't know what plants combine well to add the sizzle they desire in their landscape. With the help of this book, you'll be able to see dazzling plant partners that work well together in various seasons and in many styles of gardens, from cottage to tropical to herb to butterfly and hummingbird gardens.

The good news is that there's nothing really tricky about creating a border with dazzling plant combinations. Like children playing together harmoniously because they have similar interests, plants perform well together because of their corresponding soil, water, and light requirements. If any one of these is not the same, then there is really no partnership. Shade-loving plants like hostas and impatiens are not good partners for the sun-loving lantanas and marigolds. When describing location requirements in the following chapters, "full sun" means a minimum of 8 hours of direct sunlight per day, "part sun" means 4 hours of direct sunlight, and "shade" means approximately 2 hours of direct sunlight.

Soil Preparation Is the Key to a Green Thumb

In today's modern neighborhoods, it seems that most of the good topsoil has been scraped off and some fill is brought in for the foundation of the home. The surrounding soils may do a fair job in keeping the foundation level and resistant to shifting, but it is hardly fit for plants like shrubs and surely not flowers.

Roots of bedding plants have to penetrate soils quickly, anchor the plants, and absorb water, nutrients, and oxygen, often under adverse conditions. Soil texture plays the most important role in determining whether these needs are met sufficiently to allow the plant to become established and perform to expectations. Desirable soil holds water while allowing for proper drainage. It also provides adequate oxygen for root growth.

Tight and heavy clay soils do not provide good drainage and air circulation, whereas excessively sandy soils dry quickly and allow for rapid leaching of nutrients. For those gardeners who do not have good topsoil, amending the planting area is one of the best ways to have success. Add organic matter such as fine pine bark (pieces less than ½ inch), leaf mold, compost, and peat. For clayey soils, incorporating a 3- to 4-inch layer of organic matter with a little sand to the soil allows the bed to be built up, while improving soil texture, workability, and drainage. For sandy soils, adding organic matter will greatly improve the water- and nutrient-holding capacity

Raised-Bed Gardening Makes the Job Easier

Twenty years ago if you mentioned raised bed gardening, probably what would have come to mind was railroad or landscape timbers encompassing a vegetable garden. But today, many gardeners are growing flowers and shrubs in raised beds. From the standpoint of flowers, the ultimate raised bed is a large container filled with a good light potting mix and several species of flowers. Visualize a flowerbed as a pot about 8 to 10 inches high and perhaps covering 100 square feet. In other words, a raised flowerbed should be like a large horizontal pot.

First, clear the bed area of vegetation. Depending on the depth of the enclosure, tilling the underlying ground may or may not have to be done. Raised flowerbeds are often separated from turf areas by baked enamel edging, heavy-duty vinyl, timbers, pavers, or stones. To fill the bed, bring in a prepared landscape planting mix or blend, which may contain composted bark, sand, mushroom compost, cotton burr compost, and topsoil. Regardless of the components, the soil should be loose for young plants. Such planting media can be purchased in bags at garden centers or in bulk from local producers.

Separating raised beds from turf areas makes a lot of sense. From an aesthetic standpoint, the flowers or shrubs stand out and the grass looks better. Separating the plants is also good from a maintenance perspective. Plants grown in beds normally don't have the same water requirements as turf areas, and zoned irrigation can be easily set up. But the real ease comes from using a string trimmer or edger around the bed's wall, which will take minutes versus the hours needed to get rid of grass growing among the flowers if no barrier were present.

Raised bed gardening provides the best environment for plants and puts the joy back in planting flowers and shrubs. Because plants do better in raised beds, your money will be wisely invested. With this accomplished you can begin the task of selecting flowers.

Comprehending Color

My family owned a semi-weekly newspaper in Texas, which is where I first got fascinated with color. There was something magical about how the three primary colors could be mixed to produce every conceivable hue. As the pressman made his adjustments, a little more color here, a little less there, what was known as process color was achieved. I must state for the record, however, that as a teenager I found no redeeming value in cleaning the press afterward.

In grade school we learned that red, yellow, and blue are the three primary colors, those colors that cannot be made by any combination of other colors. The three primary colors can be combined to make the three secondary colors, orange (red and yellow), green (yellow and blue), and purple (blue and red). Finally, the primary colors can be combined with the secondary colors to form six tertiary colors, yellow-orange, red-orange, red-purple, blue-purple, blue-green, and yellow-green. Understanding the tertiary colors really helps in creating the most stunning gardens. These twelve colors make up the artist color wheel that has become a standard in garden design books. As you start to work with your flower bed or border and think of the array of colors, there's no need to stress and let your heart start to palpitate. There are a few simple concepts to keep in mind as you choose color combinations.

Monochromatic Color Schemes

Think about the last time you chose paint colors. You picked out several cards, chips, or swatches with color choices. The cards likely had several shades of the same color. If you chose two or three colors from the same card, you were using a monochromatic color scheme, blends of the same color. The monochromatic color scheme is an almost foolproof way to not make a mistake in the landscape. It's also absolutely guaranteed to make you look like you knew what you were doing. In fact, many of your neighbors will suspect you broke down and hired a professional landscape firm. Color used in a monochromatic scheme also creates spaciousness, because it is not broken or interrupted by another color.

A good place to start is with your favorite color. This is the real you; it's a color you are passionate about. If you're thinking, "Single-color plantings are boring," you best get that out of your head. You may opt for blends of the same color, but this doesn't mean all the same flower. When using a monochromatic scheme, plan on using as many different heights, shapes, and textures as possible. For instance, consider how dazzling a planting could be using 'Sparkler Violet' cleome with exotic spider-like blossom that reaches 3 to 4 feet tall. In front of the cleome, you might use 'Salsa' salvia in the same violet shades only darker and richer. Then in front plant some ground-hugging spreading petunias in shades of violet. The plants in this combination are

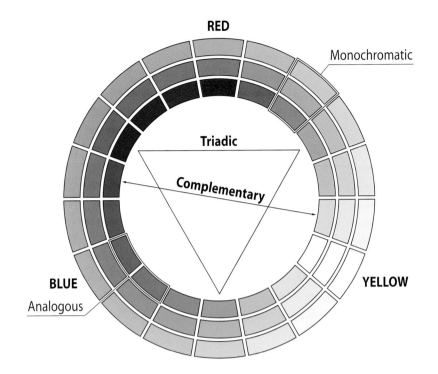

RED

Monochromatic

Triadic

Complementary

BLUE

YELLOW

Analogous

tall, medium, and prostrate and have different flower structures—delicate long stamens on the cleome, spikes on the salvia, and round blooms on the petunia.

No matter where you start on a color wheel, on the hot side of reds and yellows or the cool side of blues, you can rest assured that there are plants available for you to create your blend and design. Although the monochromatic color scheme has strong characteristics, most gardeners opt for using several colors. Sometimes gardeners use a polychromatic scheme that uses every color imaginable. Though such a garden will certainly be colorful, more than likely it will look as though there was no planning involved. When a little order is put to the design, more satisfactory results are likely to occur. If the monochromatic scheme is not for you, consider these other combinations.

Analogous Color Scheme

The analogous color scheme uses colors next to each other on the color wheel: red and orange, orange and yellow, yellow and green, green and blue, blue and violet, and violet and red. Typically one color is more dominant in the planting combination. As you choose analogous colors, make sure there is adequate contrast between them. This scheme is not rigid, in that colors do not have to be exactly next to each other but very close, for instance, red and yellow would be a suitable analogous combination.

Complementary Color Scheme

Contrast is what this scheme is all about. Complementary colors are quite different but they bring out the best in each other. In creating a complementary color scheme one color comes from the hot side of the wheel and the other is its direct opposite from the cool side. Examples are red and green, orange and blue, and yellow and violet. An exciting variation of this is called the split complementary color scheme. Once the dominant color is chosen, colors next to the direct opposite are selected. This scheme gives you an extra color while still having high contrast.

Triadic or Quadratic Color Scheme

As you get more comfortable with the combinations, consider choosing three or four colors that are spaced equal distance apart on the wheel. Triadic or quadratic color schemes have strong contrast but preserve balance and color vibrancy. These are not as contrasting as the complementary scheme but close, and they do exhibit more balance and harmony. These schemes give you more color to work with and an opportunity to use a greater variety of plants.

Rousing Red

Red is the color choice of children. Santa Claus wears red. Red stimulates excitement and passion. If your mate is seeing red, you're probably headed for the spare bedroom, couch, or worse. On Valentine's Day the heart-shaped box of chocolates is red as well as the sexy sleepwear from Victoria's Secret. We've always believed the president had a red phone for dire emergencies, which were sure to come from the Communists or Reds. Shoplifters are caught red handed. And when the girl kissed his cheek he turned red with embarrassment.

There is nothing subtle about the color red, and it is probably the most difficult color in which to develop a monochromatic color

scheme. Red is only red if it is saturated. Add a touch of yellow, and you get an orange hue. For a warm partnership, reds work wonderfully in combinations with orange and yellow flowers. On the other hand, mixing blue with red gives purple; mix it with white and you get pink. These combinations will then be tipped toward the cooler side of red, which partners well with pinks, blues, or violets. The key to making your garden work monochromatically with red is to use at least one saturated red flower group. Saturated red can be combined harmoniously with other flowers on the pink side or orange side, but definitely not both. Try red, pink, and maroon for a visually stimulating display.

Red's opposite is green. This makes complimentary color schemes in the garden easy because most leaves are green. For instance, a bed of 'Vista Red' salvia already has its opposite color in the leaves. But red doesn't have to come from flowers; 'Molten Lava' red coleus and 'Big Blonde' green coleus can be combined for a breathtaking display of foliage.

Red used in triadic displays are visually thrilling. In this scheme, red, blue, and yellow equally distanced on the color wheel work much like a soprano, tenor, and alto would in music. In the patriotic style garden, the old red, white, and blue work together much like a triadic combination, with white acting in the role of yellow.

Flamboyant Orange

On the color wheel, orange is between yellow and red and is the hallmark color of the hot side of the wheel. Orange in the garden cannot be overlooked. It just reaches out and grabs you. A complimentary pairing with blue is a marriage made in gardening heaven, but orange can stand and dazzle all on its own.

If you have only a small area for planting, orange could be the color to use, as no other color would be showier for a pocket type planting. If orange sounds too bold, you can always tone it down by using its cousins apricot, coral, and salmon.

Mention orange in the garden and the first thought may be lantanas, zinnias, or rudbeckias, all of which are known for enduring long hot summers in the sun. But we should never underestimate the effect of orange and all its relatives in shady areas. The shade garden can go relatively unnoticed or undefined, but add some orange or

apricot and look out. We think of the shade garden as cooler because of the lack of light. When we place orange there, we mentally warm it up.

For a long season of orange tones in the shade garden, your first consideration must be impatiens. There are so many to choose from that you can literally hand-select shades of orange and flower shapes like traditional single petal, semi-double, or the perfect rose form. We can even choose the exotic looking New Guinea impatiens. Every year I am amazed by the colors still showing in early autumn when gardeners have kept their impatiens watered and fed through the long summer. The show in the landscape almost rivals the azalea bloom.

Another must to consider for the summer shade garden is the begonia. The award-winning 'Dragon Wing Red' is actually on the orange side of the scale. No begonia is prettier or easier to grow in the landscape or container. Many begonia series have flowers bordering on orange.

Lastly, don't forget about orange foliage for the shade garden. When I think of colorful orange leaves, coleus comes to mind. These can add a tropical touch and can be used with ferns or hostas. Don't be afraid to partner them with impatiens. I love the selections called 'Rustic Orange', 'Freckles', and 'Stained Glassworks Copper'.

Cheerful Yellow

If there were a color that represented happiness in the garden, it would have to be yellow. One of the three primary colors, yellow has the power to evoke hope and excitement. When the forsythia breaks forth in the early spring, it not only catches your eye but invigorates your step. Winter is over and a new season has begun. On a bigger scale, yellow can make a large landscape seem cozier.

Yellow is on the hot side of the color wheel and offers warmth like the radiating sun. A pocket of yellow flowers at an entrance will give a warm welcome to visitors. If you use yellow near what might be considered a blemish or weakness in the landscape, then everyone's eye will be drawn there. There's a reason the school bus and road signs are yellow: it draws attention.

With yellow, you can really play with the amount of color saturation. The more saturated the yellows, the warmer the feel. Bright yel-

low tulips or daffodils partnered with pansies warm the early-spring garden. Conversely, pastel yellows like the yarrow, Jerusalem sage, or 'Moonbeam' coreopsis, though cheerful, buffer the intense summer heat.

The shade garden that seems to go unnoticed can be given a new vibrant feel with yellow flowers like the Fusion Glow series of exotic impatiens or by using foliage with golden yellow shades. Hostas offer a lot of choices of yellow in the shade garden.

Deeper darker yellows are found slightly to the warmer side of yellow. This seems to be where the real troopers for summer-long color are found, plants like 'New Gold' lantana, 'Million Gold' melampodium, and 'Indian Summer' rudbeckia.

Yellow's complementary color is violet or purple. When you partner the color of royalty with the radiant and gleaming yellow, there's a pageantry that manifests itself in the garden. Try the ANGELFACE series of angelonias with melampodium or 'Wildfire Violet' verbena with 'New Gold' lantana. Don't forget about blue either. Though not opposite, yellow and blue combine wonderfully and enhance each other like a couple of spouses who have been married for years. Try pairings of 'Goldsturm' rudbeckia and 'Sunny Border Blue' veronica or 'Prairie Sun' rudbeckia and 'Victoria Blue' salvia.

Yellow works exceedingly well with its neighbors, orange and red. 'Zenith Red and Gold' marigold, 'Sizzler Red' salvia, 'Fresh Look Red' celosia, and 'Swizzle Scarlet and Yellow' zinnias are all incredible plants that perform all season long.

Luscious Green

I once gave a presentation at a prestigious gardening symposium on the use of color. I might add that I thought I did very well. The next speaker got up and told the audience they didn't need color. Green is the only color you need. Let color come from your friends and visitors. I was really amused and appreciated his presentation, because green is the mandatory color in the garden. Without green, our garden is a like a desert or Siberian wasteland. Before any color can be planted, the bones or foundation from green must be in place. Keep in mind that the main color during the dormant season is green.

Green is lush and mentally cooling when used in the summer landscape. Of course, large green plants actually do cool, which is one

reason for the widespread planting of trees in cities across the United States. If you ever have the opportunity to go to a tropical rainforest, you must do so. There is green everywhere—gigantic green, to be exact. But the green serves as the backdrop for heliconias, orchids, and bromeliads. Their colors are intensified against the green. Green can also serve as a transition color, tying the garden together when you might otherwise have a clashing of color. It's like a mediator between rivals, bringing tranquility to the garden. Green harmonizes with just about every color you can think of, including members of its own family. Hostas come in a range of greens, from yellow green to blue green, including many with variegation.

In recent years, lime green or chartreuse has become very popular in the garden world. This color should be used sparingly, like a necklace holding sapphires. Chartreuse brightens the shade garden. It is so tropical looking and shouts "look at me."

Cool Blue

The word *blue* can invoke different feelings or thoughts because it carries a lot of meanings in the English language. Blue in the U.S. flag is the color of the chief, signifying vigilance, perseverance, and justice. Perhaps you've said a friend is "true blue." People describe their mood as blue when they are a little depressed. The terms "blue movies" and "blue-eyed floozies" are polite ways to refer to questionable topics. Who doesn't want to swim in the clear, blue water of the Caribbean or look with envy at the neighbor's pool on a hot sunny day?

In the horticultural world, blue causes the most ridicule among plant breeders and those who name new plants. It seems I am on the shoot of our television segment at least once a year when the plant being filmed is called a blue something. The crew laughs because invariably the plant is a shade of purple. I once heard a plant breeder say that if the new flower is not orange or yellow, then they have a right to call it blue. This was obviously a tongue-in-cheek effort to poke fun at this naming game.

Blue catches the eye when used in the garden, and it's a color that all gardeners treasure. It is the ultimate cool color. Blue is unique in that if it is mixed with a hint of another color, you still have a shade of blue. These blue shades all work harmoniously with each other. Blue also works with any other color in the garden. Its opposite is

orange, and this may be the most wonderful marriage in gardening. Put it with red and white, and you have a patriotic garden.

Everyone enjoys the old-fashioned larkspurs, standing so erect as they kick off spring with their riotous shades of blue. For summer, I love blue salvias like 'Victoria Blue', the award-winning 'Evolution' mealycup sage, and the 'Mystic Spires Blue' salvia. Blue petunias like 'Easy Wave Blue', 'Suncatcher Sapphire', and 'Sanguna Atomic Blue' also make wonderful additions to any garden. Almost every verbena series has some great blues. Look for the Aztec, Tapien, Temari, Tukana, and Wildfire series. For rock-solid, tough-as-nails, summer-long blue, you can't beat scaevola, the fan flower from Australia. For the shade garden, consider blue-foliage hosta selections.

Purples and violets will start to disappear with sunset, but blue plants like scaevola, 'Biloxi Blue' verbena, and even spiderwort almost glow iridescently just before dark. It's because our eyes are more sensitive to blues at dusk.

Royalty's Violet

Violet is the darkest on the color wheel and is the color closest to black. Violet is the color of royalty, as it looks rich and expensive. Soldiers injured in war are given a Purple Heart. Sometimes violet is thought of as a moody color. Children love purple as it's associated with grapes, jelly, and juice.

I used my favorite search engine and asked the question, "What is the difference between violet and purple?" The number of answers I got indicated to me there are a lot of people with too much time on their hands. I also found scientific papers on the subject, including one called "Purple, the Fake Color" that was based on chromaticity diagrams. Another paper dealt with a crayon company selling a particular color called violet (purple). One of my favorite garden books probably gives the best answer, "Add the slightest hint of red to violet and you tip the scale toward purple; add even more and you'll get magenta."

Flowers with a violet color may be a little submissive in the garden. They tend to disappear in the shadows or at sunset, but they can harmonize well with other colors. Violet dazzles when partnered with the complementary yellow. The garden will come alive when you combine violets with pinks. Use violet with blues and it will look like

you hired a landscape professional. Don't forget the softer versions of violets that we tend to call lavender or lilac.

The first cool front in autumn triggers pansy- and viola-planting mania. There are some incredible violets or purples to choose from, such as 'Angel Violet Duet' viola, which is the perfect flower to show the subtle differences between violet and purple. The outer petals have a very slight touch of red to make purple, while the inner petals are a true violet. The look of these fragrant, cool-season blossoms is absolutely stunning. In summer, we can select flowers like 'ANGELFACE Dark Violet' angelonia or summer snapdragon. This selection is by far the darkest angelonia on the market. It's also vigorous, sending up a bounty of wonderfully spiky flowers that are so welcome in the garden. 'Panola Deep Purple' pansy has become a favorite for its color and longevity in the garden.

Glistening White

White represents purity, which goes in hand with the bride wearing a white dress or the nurse wearing a white uniform. In the morning you wake to see pure white snow on the ground that hasn't been violated in any way. When spring arrives each year with all of its glorious colors, the one guaranteed to catch your eye every time is white. Of course, technically white is not a color, but a lack of color. White objects reflect all wavelengths of light.

Notice what Mother Nature does in the forest. The dogwoods blooms seem to glow, attracting our attention to the glistening, reflective bracts in an otherwise dull forest. White flowers not only give definition to those shadier areas of the landscape, but also offer a sense of cleanliness and purity. They also give a feeling of planning and precision, as if the gardener knew what he was doing by carefully planting white.

Notice I said "carefully." While some argue that every other color looks its best partnered with white, other colors can also be overwhelmed. White is so flashy and bright it can steal the promise or potential of its companions. In the section on grasses, notice how the tiny white flowers of 'Diamond Frost' euphorbia enhances the look of all its companions.

The reflective capacity of white is what makes it so outstanding. Every gardener loves azaleas, and the Southern Indica types like

'Formosa', 'Judge Solomon', and 'George Lindley Taber' are some of the most popular. But in the garden late in the afternoon, those purple, pink, and lavender azalea flowers start to drop out of sight, while the white-flowered Southern Indica 'G.G. Gerbing' is still glistening. This is one of the best old-time white azaleas around. The large white pom-pom flowers of the Chinese snowball viburnum make an incredible partnership with azaleas.

White is the last color to disappear as the sun sets in the evening. If it is a moonlit night, then white flowers will reflect this light all night. Use flowering vines like the moonflower to add nighttime interest and fragrance. When possible use white bedding plants at the front of the border and along sidewalks or trails to define where the walkway begins. This makes the nighttime garden come alive.

The Captivating Combinations

In this book you'll find combinations demonstrating virtually all of the color schemes, including some that maybe stretch the typical definitions. Most books on combinations deal strictly with the art side of how colors work together. Instead, I address the partnerships by style or theme, such as tropical, butterfly, cottage, and patriotic. Other sections are dedicated to combinations that were made more beautiful or striking because they included a particular type of plant, such as a grass or foliage. These days almost everyone gardens in containers, whether they have an acre or live in an apartment with a balcony. Here you'll see that the thriller, spiller, and filler recipe is one for success. With the help of this book you will be able to see these dazzling partners together and know in what season they should perform. It won't be long until you see cars slowing down in front of your home. Don't be alarmed as these passersby enviously peer out the window, they are just looking at your captivating combinations.

Complementary

Gardeners wanting to quickly and easily maximize interest in the flower border should consider using the complementary color scheme, which is based on the idea that opposites attract. Their contrast is considered the key relationship. In Chinese food it's sweet and sour sauce, and in iced tea it's lemon and sugar. In flower combinations it's about hot and cold. One color comes from the hot side of the color wheel and the other is directly opposite on the cool side.

The complementary color scheme also offers the ability to create a show with your home's exterior color. Today's newer homes are mostly neutral, but homes in historical neighborhoods tend to have striking colors of the period. If you are lucky enough to live in a colorful house, then you have the opportunity to use flowers complementing the paint scheme.

A complementary color has everything its opposite lacks. Consider the radiance presented by the color yellow. A totally yellow landscape would be like sitting in the sun all day. After a while in this garden you begin to feel a little depleted, your mind begins to try and temper the flame. This is where the color purple would come in. It offers soothing to the spirit. Darker violet is often referred to as a moody color, but place it with its opposite the cheerful yellow and you have a combination that is hard to beat.

The Christmas season is designed around another such contrast, red and its opposite green: red holly berries and green leaves on the mantle, red ribbons tied to the green tree. In the garden the deeply saturated red salvia has its own contrasting partner in its foliage. Orange and blue is another complementary scheme.

As you design with the complementary color scheme, don't just focus on flowers. Your garden center also has a wide selection of plants grown for colorful foliage. Try creating dazzling combinations with foliage plants like coleus, copper plant, setcreasea, and Persian shield. Many of these

colorful leafed plants have some of the longer seasons of performance, offering great value for your garden budget.

If you are selecting plants for a small or pocket-type planting, which are great for your most important places like an entryway, a couple of different plant textures will suffice. An example might be yellow tulips and 'Panola Deep Purple' pansies. But as you develop a larger flower border, use several different species and textures in each color to keep the garden lively.

Bouquets Galore

If you want bouquets for indoors, this is the plant partnership for you. 'Bouquet Purple' dianthus, a great landscape performer, produces flower stalks reaching 18 to 24 inches in height. The flowers are a bright and bold hot purple-pink. Toughness is another outstanding attribute, as 'Bouquet Purple' has won awards from Minnesota to Mississippi. Its partner 'Early Sunrise' coreopsis is also an award winner. *Coreopsis grandiflora* is native to North America and offers brilliant golden-yellow flowers borne on 2-foot-long stems.

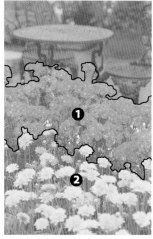

1 'Bouquet Purple' dianthus (*Dianthus barbatus* interspecific hybrid 'Bouquet Purple'), zones 4–9

2 'Early Sunrise' coreopsis (*Coreopsis grandiflora* 'Early Sunrise'), zones 4–9

Location: full sun, fertile well-drained soil

Growing tip: Deadheading or removing of spent blossoms is important. It keeps flowers producing and lessens disease pressure.

Season of performance: spring and summer

1 'Goldsturm' rudbeckia
(*Rudbeckia fulgida* var. *sulli-vantii* 'Goldsturm'), zones 3–8

2 'Sunny Border Blue'
veronica (*Veronica spicata*
hybrid 'Sunny Border Blue'),
zones 3–8

Location: full sun, fertile
well-drained soil

Growing tip: Keep the
plants deadheaded for
autumn color and divide
after about 4 years.

Season of performance:
summer through autumn

Double Distinction

This partnership is so alluring because of the contrasting golden orange and violet blue. It's also stunning because you have round flowers with those that are vertically inclined. Despite these marked contrasts, rudbeckia and veronica also have a couple of common features. Both of these flowers won the coveted Perennial Plant of the Year Award from the Perennial Plant Association. This combination is also well suited to the backyard wildlife habitat as the plants attract bees, birds, and butterflies.

Exploring the Globe

Although the violet-colored balls of 'All Around Purple' gomphrena look like tasty grape gumdrops ready for munching, they are among the toughest flowers in the summer landscape. Sometimes called globe amaranth or bachelor's button, they are excellent flowers for cutting and drying. They complement the 'Bonanza Yellow' marigolds for months of color. 'Explorer' petunias spread to 3 feet. Here their pink flowers work in harmony with the taller gomphrena to create a colorful bouquet-like bed with the marigolds.

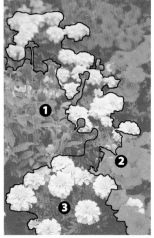

1 'All Around Purple' gomphrena (*Gomphrena globosa* 'All Around Purple'), annual

2 'Explorer Rose Pink' petunia (*Petunia* 'Explorer Rose Pink'), annual

3 'Bonanza Yellow' marigold (*Tagetes patula* 'Bonanza Yellow'), annual

Location: full sun, fertile well-drained soil

Growing tip: Keep the gomphrena and marigolds deadheaded for increased blooming. Cut back petunias in late summer to rejuvenate growth and blooms.

Season of performance: spring through summer

Fire and Ice Crescendo

1 Yellow tulip (*Tulipa* cv.), annual, perennial in zones 3–6

2 'Panola Golden Yellow' and 'Panola Deep Purple' pansy (*Viola* x *wittrockiana* 'Panola Golden Yellow' and 'Panola Deep Purple'), annuals

Location: full sun, fertile well-drained soil rich with organic matter

Growing tip: Inter-planting spring bulbs isn't just for a complementary color schemes, but for monochromatic and multicolored triadic or quadratic partnering as well.

Season of performance: spring

Fiery yellow and cool purple 'Panola' pansies contrast in a dazzling fashion that no doubt has looked good for months prior to the arrival of spring bulb season. But like an orchestra with a climaxing crescendo, the emergence of the yellow tulips brings the garden to its spring peak. It won't be long until these annuals are switched to warm-season performers.

Fragrant Fire

'Citrona Orange' erysimum is the colorful pansy partner you've long wanted. This member of the cabbage family sends up spikes loaded with flaming orange or brilliant yellow flowers that have a tantalizing fragrance. The 'Citrona' will be winter hardy from zones 7 to 11, so it can be planted in the previous autumn. In this dazzling combination planting, the 'Citrona' orange is combined with its cool complement, the large-flowered 'Matrix Blue Blotch' pansy. The Matrix series has become widely recognized for its dazzling landscape performance and durability.

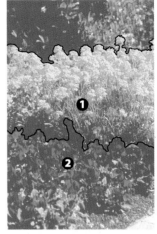

1 'Citrona Orange' erysimum (*Erysimum* 'Citrona Orange'), annual

2 'Matrix Blue Blotch' pansy (*Viola* x *wittrockiana* 'Matrix Blue Blotch'), annual

Location: full to part sun, fertile well-drained soil

Growing tip: Pansies with splashes of rusty burgundy or mahogany are also stunning partners for 'Citrona Orange'.

Season of performance: autumn and spring in the South, spring and summer in the North

From Russia with Love

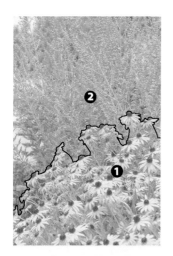

Like 'Goldsturm', the Russian sage also garnered the Perennial Plant of the Year award from the Perennial Plant Association and has been a favorite ever since. With its airy to wispy structure, olive gray foliage, and violet blue flowers, Russian sage softens the flashy boldness of 'Goldsturm', making a very appealing marriage. Both flowers have a strong appeal to bees and butterflies, although the pungent aroma of the Russian sage's leaves makes it deer resistant.

1 'Goldsturm' rudbeckia (*Rudbeckia fulgida* var. *sullivantii* 'Goldsturm'), zones 3–8

2 Russian sage (*Perovskia atriplicifolia*), zones 4–9

Location: full sun, fertile well-drained soil

Growing tip: As spring approaches, cut the plants back to just above ground level. Divide in the early spring with the emergence of new growth.

Season of performance: summer through autumn

Fruitful Fragrance

'Velocity Lemon and Plum Picotee' viola offers its own version of the complementary color scheme without even having a partner. Of course, that's one of the reasons pansies and violas are so loved. Although violas have a delightful fragrance, add 'Vanilla Sachet' nemesia to the mix and you'll come under the spell of the smell. Use in containers, too, near places you frequent during the cool season. Nemesia is related to the snapdragon and planted in the same season: autumn in the South or spring in the North.

1 'Velocity Lemon and Plum Picotee' viola (Viola cornuta 'Velocity Lemon and Plum Picotee'), annual

2 'Vanilla Sachet' nemesia (Nemesia 'Sachet Vanilla'), annual

Location: full sun, fertile soil rich with organic matter

Growing tip: Pansies and violas are heavy feeders, so give frequent applications of dilute water-soluble fertilizer.

Season of performance: autumn through spring in the South, spring and summer in the North

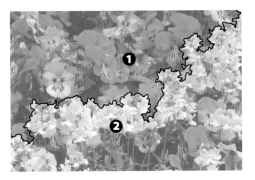

Gaudy but Great

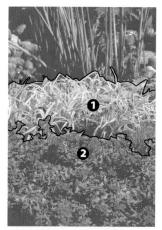

'Sweet Kate' fits perfectly with the latest trend of chartreuse and lime green. The foliage is so colorful you don't care if it blooms. But guess what, it does. The blooms of 'Sweet Kate' are an eye-catching, complementary violet blue, so the flowers make a perfect partner with the foliage. Spiderworts are known for toughness and some even aggressiveness. Here its picturesque partner is the rugged 'Homestead Purple' verbena, which has received awards throughout the country. This verbena spreads outward up to 3 feet.

1 'Sweet Kate'
tradescantia or spiderwort
(*Tradescantia* 'Sweet Kate'),
zones 4–11

2 'Homestead Purple'
verbena (*Verbena canadensis* 'Homestead Purple'),
annual, perennial in zones
6–9

Location: full sun, fertile
well-drained soil

Growing tip: Cut back the
verbena in the summer
once the cycle of blooms
starts to end, and apply a
little fertilizer.

Season of Performance:
late spring and summer

Glowing Lavender

**1 'Million Gold' melam-
podium**
(Melampodium divaricatum
'Million Gold'), annual

**2 'Madness Lavender
Glow' petunia** (Petunia
'Madness Lavender Glow'),
annual

Location: full sun, fertile
well-drained soil

Growing tip: Expect
'Million Gold' to do a
little reseeding, giving you
another performance next
season.

Season of performance:
spring and summer

This bed has the power to draw the eye of everyone who comes near thanks to the 'Madness Lavender Glow' petunia with its almost iridescent color. 'Million Gold' melampodium might be considered the perfect plant for novices. It's just too easy to grow. We all want easy and carefree, and melampodium certainly fills the bill. This complementary marriage is sensational. You can't get this look from just a six-pack of plants, so plant a lot of them.

Green-eyed Girl

A mass planting of 'Prairie Sun' is a sight not soon forgotten. Though commonly known as a black-eyed Susan, 'Prairie Sun' might best be called the "green-eyed girl" for the round center disk. The large flowers are orange with yellow-tipped petals. 'Prairie Sun' is great for cutting and attracts birds and butterflies. The orange and yellow blends complement the frosty blue and white 'Strata' mealycup sage. Both plants fit the cottage garden, butterfly garden, or wildflower meadow garden.

1 'Prairie Sun' black-eyed Susan (Rudbeckia hirta 'Prairie Sun'), zones 3–8

2 'Strata' mealycup sage (Salvia farinacea 'Strata'), annual, perennial in zones 7–10

Location: full sun, fertile well-drained soil

Growing tip: Buy young transplants with no buds. Prompt deadheading will keep this bed performing for a long time.

Season of performance: summer through autumn

Photo courtesy of Terry Howe, Ball Horticultural Co.

Icy Hot

The Profusion series has brought fun back to growing zinnias. They are tough, disease resistant, and packed with color. The icy blue flowers of the 'Blue Daze' evolvulus, while not directly opposite to orange, are close enough to make a standout combination, coupling beauty and toughness. Unfortunately, many gardeners aren't familiar with 'Blue Daze'. It's in the morning glory family but stays compact, reaching about 1 foot tall with a spread of 2 to 3 feet. The leaves are covered in gray fuzz, adding even more texture to the garden.

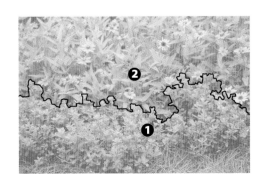

Not to Be Out-Phloxed

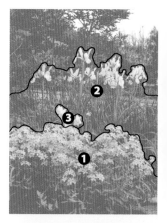

Woodland phlox makes the spring garden literally come alive with fragrance and rare shades of lavender and blue. Called Louisiana phlox in the South, woodland phlox is native over a wide area of the United States. The plant makes exceptional combinations with azaleas, dogwoods, and redbuds. It also makes sense to partner woodland phlox with spring bulbs, as in this garden. The 'Wedgwood' Dutch iris is simply exquisite as a partner. The daffodils, with their yellow trumpets, contrast wonderfully with the blue of the phlox and strengthen the yellow in the iris.

1 Woodlands phlox (Phlox divaricata), zones 4–9

2 'Wedgwood' Dutch iris (Iris 'Wedgwood'), zones 5–8

3 Daffodil (Narcissus cv.), zones 5–8

Location: full sun, fertile well-drained soil rich with organic matter

Growing tip: Correcting fertility is a challenge once perennials have become established, so do it prior to planting.

Season of performance: spring

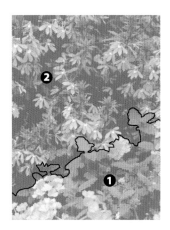

1 'Lanai Peach' verbena
(Verbena 'Lanai Peach'),
annual, perennial in zones
7–10

**2 'Bombay Blue' fan
flower** (Scaevola aemula
'Bombay Blue'), annual,
perennial in zones 9–11

Location: full to part sun,
fertile well-drained soil

Growing tip: Don't hesi-
tate to cut the verbena back
a couple of times during
the growing season to generate growth and blooms.

Season of performance:
spring through autumn

Peachy Partner

Peach is a rare color in the garden and creating a partnership worthy of a
photograph is even more difficult. When you see 'Lanai Peach' verbena and
'Bombay Blue' scaevola together, your first thought might be, "Why didn't
I think of that?" This hybrid verbena is considered an annual, although it
may return in spring in zones 7–10 provided the winter drainage is good.
'Bombay Blue' fan flower blooms from the moment you buy it until frost
kills it in the autumn.

Picture of Perfume

'Velocity Purple Bicolor' viola demonstrates the extraordinary colors and flower power available from violas and shows that bigger is not always better. These plants are extremely cold tolerant and have shown remarkable heat tolerance once spring starts to retreat. This garden is not only exquisitely beautiful, contrasting from the pristine white, but also delightfully scented. The violas are fragrant and with the 'Sachet Vanilla' nemesias are absolutely tantalizing. Nemesias are related to snapdragons and perform during the same season.

1 'Velocity Purple Bicolor' viola (Viola cornuta 'Velocity Purple Bicolor'), annual

2 'Sachet Vanilla' nemesia (Nemesia 'Sachet Vanilla'), annual

Location: full to part sun, fertile well-drained soil rich with organic matter

Growing tip: Violas are heavy feeders, so feed every 2 or 3 weeks with a diluted, water-soluble fertilizer.

Season of performance: autumn through spring in the South, spring and summer in the North

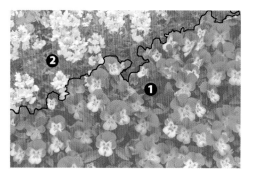

Singing the Blues

**1 'Panola True Blue'
pansy** (Viola xwittrockiana
'Panola True Blue'), annual

**2 'Sorbet Peach Frost'
viola** (Viola cornuta 'Sorbet
Peach Frost'), annual

Location: full sun, fertile
soil rich with organic matter

Growing tip: Cold fronts
often have a drying effect,
so pay attention to mois-
ture needs.

Season of performance:
autumn through spring in
the South, spring through
midsummer in the North

'Panola True Blue', a medium-sized pansy, has almost iridescent, electric
blue flowers. Partner it with 'Sorbet Peach Frost' viola, and the phrase "singing the blues" will have a new meaning. With genetics from both violas
and pansies, the Panola series has a lot of flowers and remarkable heat
tolerance. 'Sorbet Peach Frost' has a healthy dose of the same blue as the
'Panola True Blue', but complemented with a splash of creamy yellow and
hot orange.

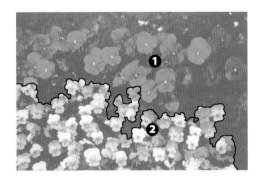

**1 'SunBathers Gold Coast'
gazania** (Gazania 'SunBathers Gold Coast'), annual,
perennial in zones 8–11

**2 'Cascadia Improved
Charlie' petunia** (Petunia
'Cascadia Improved Char-
lie'), annual

Location: full sun, fertile
well-drained soil

Growing tip: The gazania
needs consistent moisture
without overwatering.
Deadhead to get repeat
blooms. Cut back petunias
in late summer to generate
new growth and blooms.

Season of performance:
summer through autumn

Sunbathing with Charlie

Native to Africa, 'SunBathers Gold Coast' gazania has caused quite a com-
motion, with its extra large semi-double flowers and without the typical
dark eye of other gazanias. The semi-double nature prevents the flowers
from closing at night, as is typical of many gazanias. The brilliant flaming
gold of the 10-inch-tall flowers is the perfect complement to the rich blue
violet of the 'Cascadia Improved Charlie' petunia. The Cascadia series are
large-flowered petunias that are both vigorous and spreading.

Sunshine on My Shoulder

This combination depicts perfectly the phrase "opposites attract." In this display, 'Loraine Sunshine' heliopsis or false sunflower appears to be placing its large golden blooms on the shoulders of the rare blue-colored geranium 'Rozanne'. The variegated white leaves with green veins of 'Loraine Sunshine' are as big an attraction as the radiant flowers. The large violet-blue flowers of 'Rozanne', with purple-violet veins and small white centers, offer nonstop flowering through the growing season. This cultivar has one of the longest flowering periods of any of the hardy geraniums.

1 'Rozanne' geranium (Geranium 'Rozanne'), zones 5–8

2 'Loraine Sunshine' false sunflower (Heliopsis helianthoides 'Loraine Sunshine'), zones 3–8

Location: full to part sun, afternoon shade in hot climates, well-drained soil

Growing tip: Cut the geranium back hard as needed to rejuvenate.

Season of performance: summer through autumn

Photo courtesy of Blooms of Bressingham

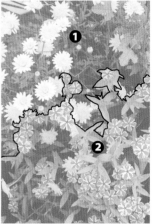

1 'Courtyard Butter-cream' marguerite daisy (*Argyranthemum frutescens* 'Courtyard Buttercream'), annual, perennial in zones 9–11

2 'Intensia Star Brite' phlox (*Phlox* 'Intensia Star Brite'), annual, perennial in zones 9–11

Location: full sun, fertile well-drained soil

Growing tip: Cutting the phlox back in late summer makes for an even more incredible autumn bloom. Frequent deadheading of the daisy will reward you with more of its colorful blossoms.

Season of performance: spring and summer

Wheels of Good Fortune

Looking through the lens of the camera at this delightful planting, it appeared as though there were colorful wheels turning in the garden. The turning appearance of the buttery creamy yellow from the 'Courtyard Buttercream' daisy was enhanced by the almost rotating purple pink pattern in the 'Intensia Star Brite' phlox. More gardeners should experience the fun of growing argyranthemum or marguerite daisy. The 'Intensia Star Brite' phlox blooms from early spring through autumn.

Wildly Lime

1 'Wild Lime' coleus (*Solenostemon scutellarioides* 'Wild Lime'), annual

2 'Prairie Sun' black-eyed Susan (*Rudbeckia hirta* 'Prairie Sun'), zones 3–8

3 'Wave Blue' petunia (*Petunia* 'Wave Blue'), annual

Location: full sun, fertile well-drained soil

Growing tip: Keep flower buds pinched on the coleus, deadhead 'Prairie Sun', and cut back petunias if needed in late summer.

Season of performance: spring and summer

You'll go wild with this combination in the landscape. Notice how the lime-green margins of the coleus pick up the green eye of 'Prairie Sun', while the yellow in the center matches the primrose yellow tips of the daisy. They are both partners in complementing the intensely colored 'Wave Blue' petunias. Opposites attract whether the plants are grown for foliage or flower.

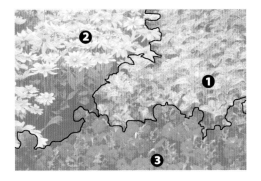

Harmony

While a complementary or contrasting color scheme works with two colors, a harmonious color scheme is larger and can be broken down into monochromatic, analogous, triadic, and quadratic color schemes.

The monochromatic color scheme uses blends of the same color and creates spaciousness because it is not broken or interrupted by another color. In this scheme, it is best to use as many different heights, shapes, and textures as possible.

Likewise, the analogous color scheme is pleasing and soothing because the colors selected are next to each other on the color wheel. There is an inherently strong relationship. It's not shocking in contrast, like the complementary scheme. Two colors will work but many suggest using three, a dominant color, one for support, and one for accent.

The final schemes are a little like singing in harmony. Many of us have had the opportunity to hear music in which soprano, alto, tenor, and bass are sung to make a magical performance. By selecting our colors equal distance apart on the color wheel, we will have a very vibrant garden with some contrast yet it is tied together in harmony through careful balance. Three colors are used for triadic harmony and four for quadratic harmony. These harmonies allow for mixing of several colors without a disruption that yields a hodgepodge appearance.

Cherry Crescendo

1 Red tulip (*Tulipa* cv.), annual, perennial in zones 3–6

2 'Panola Golden Yellow', 'Panola White', 'Panola Deep Purple', and 'Panola True Blue' pansies (*Viola xwittrockiana* Panola series), annual

Location: full sun, fertile soil rich with organic matter

Growing tip: Feed your pansies with frequent dilute applications of water-soluble fertilizer.

Season of performance: spring

What could be more exciting than driving by a colorful bed of cool-season pansies each day, and then one day red tulips are dancing above the pansies in a celebration of the change of seasons? You can duplicate this spring garden climax by inter-planting spring bulbs as you plant cool-season flowers. Bulbs like tulip, hyacinth, narcissus, and even iris can lend a celebratory spirit to the spring garden.

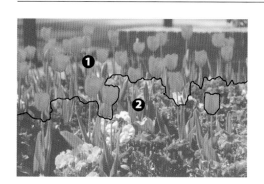

Cherry Tsunami

This trio of harmonizing colors gives you everything you could want: cherry-colored blooms that will stop traffic, blue salvias with a spiky texture that creates excitement by breaking the horizontal plane, and green-eyed gloriosa daisies perfect for cutting. The Tidal Wave series of petunias gives billowing seas of color and brings a new class of petunia to the garden called hedgiflora because of their ability to form a low-growing hedge.

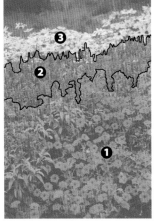

1 'Tidal Wave Cherry' petunia (*Petunia* 'Tidal Wave Cherry'), annual

2 'Evolution' mealycup sage (*Salvia farinacea* 'Evolution'), annual, perennial in zones 7–10

3 'Prairie Sun' black-eyed Susan (*Rudbeckia hirta* 'Prairie Sun'), zones 3–8

Location: full sun, fertile soil rich with organic matter

Growing tip: Deadhead salvias and rudbeckias to keep flowers producing and maintain a tidy look. Cut petunias back to induce growth and blooming in late summer.

Season of performance: spring through autumn

Enchanted Spring

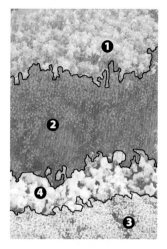

'Swan Pink and Yellow' columbine watches over this cool-season splendor. The pink enhances the darker magenta of the 'Enchantment', whose gold center plays as the richer colored foil to the primrose-colored pansies. The front of the border is massed with 'Snow Crystals' alyssum. With 'Enchantment' linaria and 'Snow Crystals' alyssum, this will be a quintessential fragrance garden asking for your participation.

1 'Swan Pink and Yellow' columbine (Aquilegia 'Swan Pink and Yellow'), annual, perennial in zones 3–8

2 'Enchantment' linaria (Linaria 'Enchantment'), annual

3 'Snow Crystals' alyssum (Lobularia maritima 'Snow Crystals'), annual

4 'Panola Silhouette Mix' pansy (Viola xwittrockiana 'Panola Silhouette Mix'), annual

Location: full sun, fertile soil rich with organic matter

Growing tip: White goes with any color, and as sunlight diminishes this white alyssum defines where the border ends and sidewalk or walkway begins.

Season of performance: spring

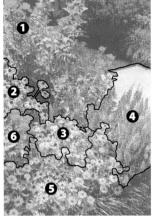

1 'Knock Out' rose (*Rosa* 'Knock Out'), zones 4–9

2 'Goldsturm' rudbeckia (*Rudbeckia fulgida* var. *sullivantii* 'Goldsturm'), zones 3–9

3 'Million Gold' melampodium (*Melampodium divaricatum* 'Million Gold'), annual

4 'Serena Purple' angelonia (*Angelonia angustifolia* 'Serena Purple'), annual, perennial in zones 9–11

5 'Profusion Fire' zinnia (*Zinnia* 'Profusion Fire'), annual

6 'Butterfly Deep Pink' pentas (*Pentas lanceolata* 'Butterfly Deep Pink'), annual, perennial in zones 9–11

Location: full sun, well-drained soil rich with organic matter

Growing tip: Deadhead, water, and feed with frequent light applications of fertilizer and this bed will perform for months.

Season of performance: summer through early autumn

Endless Summer

This garden literally stopped traffic as passersby wanted a closer look. The colors feed off one another, pushing the comfort zone in combining shrub roses, annuals, and perennials. This border is layered from back to front with transition areas and features different sizes, shapes, and textures to create interest. It also provides a welcome feast to visiting butterflies and hummingbirds.

A Fresh Approach

1 'Fresh Look Red' celosia
(*Celosia plumosa* 'Fresh Look Red'), annual

2 'Swizzle Scarlet and Yellow' zinnia (*Zinnia elegans* 'Swizzle Scarlet and Yellow'), annual

Location: full sun, fertile well-drained soil

Growing tip: Spot planting does not do the 'Fresh Look Red' justice, so plant this cultivar in masses.

Season of performance: summer and early autumn

When the intense heat of summer has us fleeing to the air conditioner, landscapes can still burst with color thanks to celosias like the 'Fresh Look Red'. It's also a popular cut flower, perfect for drying and using in floral arrangements. The 'Swizzle Scarlet and Yellow' zinnia makes an incredible partner, with the difference in texture of blooms versus plumes and the added red of the bicolor flower. Also, the colors are neighbors, giving them the ability to harmonize like a country music duet.

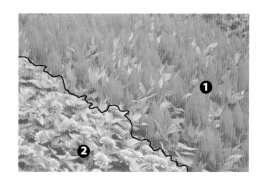

Lucky in Rio

You'll feel lucky when you partner these heat-loving flowers together because they are tough and maintenance free, allowing time for other activities. The Lucky lantana and Rio purslane series are also drought tolerant, which has become a wonderful attribute in recent summers. The yellow center on the 'Rio Scarlet' echoes the 'Lucky Yellow', while the scarlet works in an analogous relationship, making this combination a double winner. Both plants are also well suited to containers and baskets.

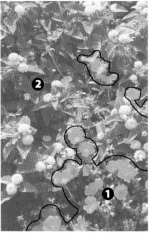

1 'Rio Scarlet' purslane
(*Portulaca oleracea* 'Rio Scarlet'), annual

2 'Lucky Yellow' lantana
(*Lantana camara* 'Lucky Yellow'), annual, perennial in zones (7) 8–11

Location: full sun, fertile well-drained soil

Growing tip: Pinching the lantana or light pruning stimulates growth and induces blooms.

Season of performance: late spring through summer

Picotee Passion

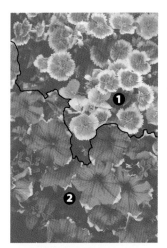

Monochromatic partners never looked so striking. This spring and summer garden shows off the two members of the close-knit color family of violet: burgundy and purple. The purple in the 'Telstar' dianthus looks to have only a very subtle difference in the burgundy of the 'Symphony' petunia. Both flowers have the tie in from white as well. The typical thought is that purples and violets are a little subdued in the garden and sometimes may go unnoticed. The white picotee, however, gives them full accord in the landscape.

1 'Telstar Purple Picotee' dianthus (*Dianthus barbatus* x *chinensis* 'Telstar Purple Picotee'), annual, perennial in zones 6–9

2 'Symphony Burgundy Picotee' petunia (*Petunia* 'Symphony Burgundy Picotee'), annual

Location: full sun, fertile well-drained soil

Growing tip: Be sure to apply a layer of mulch to keep summer soil temperatures moderate.

Season of performance: spring and summer

Pretty in Pink

'Bouquet Purple' has forever changed dianthus gardening in the United States. By offering fragrance and plenty of flowers for the vase, it earned both the Minnesota Select Perennial Plant of the Year and the Mississippi Medallion Award. Cut the long blooms and more will follow. 'Bouquet Purple' is partnered with monochromatic petunias, and 'Easter Bonnet White' alyssum generates a little contrast with white, offering fragrance as it gently tumbles over the walkway. Dusty miller is spot planted to give added textural interest.

1 'Bouquet Purple' dianthus (*Dianthus barbatus* interspecific hybrid 'Bouquet Purple'), zones 4–9

2 Petunia mix (*Petunia* cv.), annual

3 Dusty miller (*Senecio cineraria*), annual, perennial in zones 7–10

4 'Easter Bonnet White' alyssum (*Lobularia maritima* 'Easter Bonnet White'), annual

Location: full sun, fertile well-drained soil

Growing tip: Harvest 'Bouquet Purple' when three flowers in a bunch are fully opened.

Season of performance: spring through summer

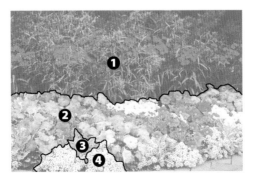

Sapphire Falls

Like a tumbling waterfall in a small stream, this trailing 'Suncatcher Sapphire' petunia creates the illusion of water flowing from the container. Suncatcher petunias are vigorous, spreading, sun-loving plants. The sapphire color has two strong partners in this planting. The most pronounced is with the red leaf of the 'Defiance' coleus. Just like a long sapphire necklace, the gold that ties the gems together is the 'Riverdene Gold' Mexican heather. The red, blue, and gold, although contrasting, form a triadic partnership.

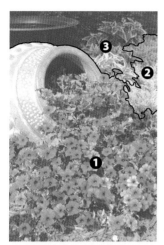

1 'Suncatcher Sapphire' petunia (Petunia 'Suncatcher Sapphire'), annual

2 'Riverdene Gold' Mexican heather (Cuphea hyssopifolia 'Riverdene Gold'), annual, perennial in zones (8) 9–11

3 'Defiance' coleus (Solenostemon scutellarioides 'Defiance'), annual

Location: full sun, fertile soil rich with organic matter

Growing tip: Keep the 'Defiance' coleus bushy and more vibrantly colored by pinching throughout the summer.

Season of performance: summer through autumn

Sea of Tranquility

Tranquil, soothing, and alluring are all appropriate adjectives for this monochromatic spring garden. If you use blends of the same color, it will look like you had a plan in mind. The trailing 'Avalanche' petunias with small but varied amounts of blue in their petals and the blue ageratums with tints of violet work perfectly to maintain this cool composition. The garden appeals not only to the visual senses but to the nose as well: the enticing fragrance of 'Wonderland Deep Purple' alyssum edging the border will make you want to linger.

1 'Avalanche' petunia (Petunia 'Avalanche'), annual

2 'Wonderland Deep Purple' alyssum (Lobularia maritima 'Wonderland Deep Purple'), annual

3 'Royal Hawaii' ageratum (Ageratum houstonianum 'Royal Hawaii'), annual

Location: full to part sun, fertile well-drained soil

Growing tip: Feed every 4 to 6 weeks and cut back to rejuvenate growth and blooms in late summer.

Season of performance: spring and summer

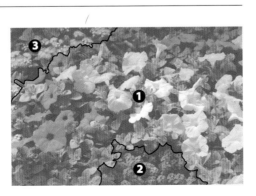

Sensory Sensation

Unparalleled beauty coupled with tantalizing fragrance makes this spring garden a place to linger and enjoy. Both the stock and the alyssum offer a delight to the olfactory senses. Stock, a relative of cabbage and kale, is grown for flowers and fragrance instead of foliage. Here the 'Hot Cakes Mix' is the focal point, forming its own monochromatic scheme in various shades of pink and rose. The white alyssum, although contrasting, gently falls over the edges to eliminate the harsh straight lines.

1 'Hot Cakes Mix' stock (Matthiola incana 'Hot Cakes Mix'), annual

2 'Clear Crystals White' alyssum (Lobularia maritima 'Clear Crystals White'), annual

Location: full to part sun, fertile well-drained soil

Growing tip: Both the stock and the alyssum make great pansy partners.

Season of performance: autumn through spring in the South, spring through midsummer in the North

Sizzling Surroundings

A massed planting of 'Sizzler Red' is enough to draw attention with its fiery scarlet, but partner it with the triploid 'Zenith Red and Gold' marigold and you have a proverbial Kodak moment. The salvia's spiky texture is most welcome in a garden world dominated by round flowers. If you have ever wondered what a cross between the African and the French marigold might look like, the 'Zenith Red and Gold' reveals the answer: awesome. Hummingbird visitors find the scarlet sage most delectable, and butterflies will love the marigolds.

1 'Sizzler Red' salvia (Salvia splendens 'Sizzler Red'), annual

2 'Zenith Red and Gold' marigold (Tagetes patula x erecta 'Zenith Red and Gold'), annual

Location: full sun, fertile well-drained soil

Growing tip: Also look for the Sunburst series of marigolds, another great triploid series.

Season of performance: spring through autumn

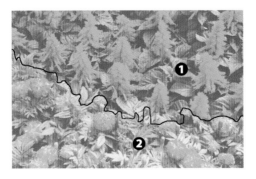

Sunrise Sensation

1 'Matrix Coastal Sunrise Mix' pansy (Viola xwittrockiana 'Matrix Coastal Sunrise Mix'), annual

2 'Swan Pink and Yellow' columbine (Aquilegia 'Swan Pink and Yellow'), annual, perennial in zones 3–8

Location: full sun, fertile soil rich with organic matter

Growing tip: Pansies are heavy feeders, so don't forget to fertilize.

Season of performance: spring in the South, spring through early summer in the North

The shades of blue in the 'Matrix Coastal Sunrise Mix' pansies are like the deep blue sea. Rose will remind you of the beginning of a new day. Then come the creams, yellows, and rusty rose of the sunrise. The pansies' partner in this remarkable display is the 24-inch-tall 'Swan Pink and Yellow' columbine. Hardy from zones 3–8, the columbine prefers cooler conditions and therefore is considered a cool-season annual in the South and a perennial in the North.

Tough Amigos

Three colors equal distance apart on the color wheel form a triad of harmony working together for maximum appeal. This combination is also comprised of plants that are tough-as-nails. When it comes to blooming and disease resistance, 'Knock Out' rose has become the one in which all others are compared. 'New Gold' lantana, one of the most awarded plants in the country, is known to bloom until frost, all the while attracting butterflies. Mexican petunia—not really a petunia at all—has blue flowers that almost glow.

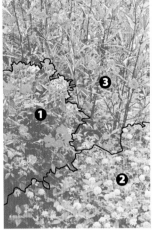

1 'Knock Out' rose (Rosa 'Knock Out'), zones 4–9

2 'New Gold' lantana (Lantana 'New Gold'), zones (7) 8–10

3 Mexican petunia (Ruellia brittoniana), annual, perennial in zones 7–10
Location: full sun, fertile well-drained soil

Growing tip: Cut 'Knock Out' back hard in late winter, and watch for unwanted volunteers of the Mexican petunia.

Season of performance: summer through autumn

Tropical

The tropical garden is about an attitude as much as it is about style. So many of us have made treks across the seas to far-off islands, where the crystal clear water, fragrant blossoms, and lush surroundings made us forget the stresses of life. Though we might have been there for weeks, time was fleeting. We find ourselves wanting to create that look and feel at home, so that when we've fought the four lanes of traffic after a contentious day at the office we can slip on some cutoffs and head to our corner of paradise in the landscape. This has become our nest, our place to cook, to unwind, to feel a little like being back on the island. Creating a tropical feel in our gardens might be as simple as adding some coarse-textured foliage in what is already a nice garden. The plants don't have to be native to the tropics. For instance, when you look at a hosta, fern, canna, elephant ear, or philodendron, you think tropical.

Many of the truly tropical plants at today's garden centers are more cold hardy than you imagined. They may freeze to the ground and return in the spring, but that's the nature of many of our regular perennials. There are bananas for sale, such as the Japanese fiber banana, that can return from −20F. In addition, many parts of the United States have a long growing season. For example, a city like Baltimore, Maryland, has around 238 days of frost-free weather and Louisville, Kentucky, has 220 days. This means for more than 7 months each year, those cities can look like Martinique.

Another good characteristic of tropical plants is their heat tolerance. When the stifling temperatures have sent you indoors, guess which plants are looking good out in the garden. More than likely they are tropical plants like lantana, mandevilla, ixora, crossandra, princess flower, and hibiscus. At these temperatures a banana plant will grow at a pace that tempts you to invite the neighbor over to watch. Try these combinations. One day you're sure to walk outside and imagine that you are hearing the distant sounds of steel drums.

Banana Flambé

The yellow forsythia sage looks like flames dancing around the giant bananas. It's not often you see salvias combined with bananas, but in this garden it has worked for years. The two Mexican salvias complement each other in color and serve as a feast for visiting ruby-throated hummingbirds. 'Kathy Ann Brown' and another called 'Santa Barbara' are shorter varieties of the Mexican bush sage.

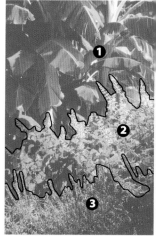

1 Plantain banana (*Musa xparadisiaca*), zones (7) 8–11

2 Forsythia sage (*Salvia madrensis*), zones 7–10

3 'Kathy Ann Brown' Mexican bush sage (*Salvia leucantha* 'Kathy Ann Brown'), zones 7b–10

Location: full sun, fertile well-drained soil

Growing tip: Good winter drainage is the key to winter survival for all three plants. Streetlights or security lights in close proximity to the salvias will most likely prevent them from blooming.

Season of performance: summer foliage, autumn bloom

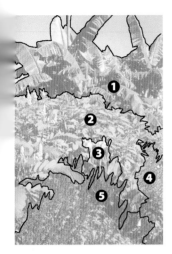

1 Plantain banana (*Musa xparadisiaca*), zones (7) 8–11

2 Candlestick plant (*Senna alata*), annual

3 'Tropical' canna (*Canna xgeneralis* 'Tropical'), zones 7–10

4 Mexican bush sage (*Salvia leucantha*), zones 7b–10

5 'Indigo Spires' salvia (*Salvia* 'Indigo Spires'), annual, perennial in zones 7–10

Location: full sun, fertile well-drained soil

Growing tip: This garden is growing on a raised bed that allows water to drain freely in the winter, which is crucial for a spring return.

Season of performance: summer and autumn

Garden of Eden

A gazebo hidden beyond these enormous banana plants provides a Caribbean-like retreat for relaxing and admiring visiting butterflies and hummingbirds. The boldly textured bananas rustle in the breeze and serve as the perfect backdrop for colorful perennials like the 'Indigo Spires' salvia and Mexican bush sage. The salvias violet and purple spiky blossoms complement the yellow candlestick plants and 'Tropical' cannas.

1 Firecracker flower (*Crossandra infundibuliformis*), annual, perennial in zones 9–11

2 Flame of the woods (*Ixora coccinea*), annual, perennial in zones 10–11

Location: full to part sun, fertile well-drained soil

Growing tip: Once the crossandra stops blooming, remove the spike to rejuvenate growth and blooming. Use this combination with philodendrons or elephant ears.

Season of performance: summer through autumn

Hot as a Firecracker

Colorful blooms that just keep coming makes flame of the woods one of the truly outstanding choices for those wanting to create the tropical garden. The genus *Ixora* is related to plants like coffee and pentas. There is a wide choice in colors, including those with multicolored blossoms, but the monochromatic orange partnership here surrounded by deep green foliage is sensational. The firecracker flower is related to the Mexican petunia and produces striking nonstop blooms on spikes topping glossy leaves.

King and Queen of the Nile

The Lily of the Nile, with its rare blue flowers, and 'King Humbert Yellow' canna, with its fiery orange, forms an exotic and complementary marriage of color, flower, and leaf texture grown from bulbs. The Lily of the Nile produces large globes (called umbels) with individual flowers numbering from 20 to more than 100. Because they open up gradually the bloom period is long, partnering well with cannas, which bloom until frost.

1 'King Humbert Yellow' canna (*Canna xgeneralis* 'King Humbert Yellow'), zones 7–10

2 Lily of the Nile agapanthus (*Agapanthus* Lily of the Nile), zones 6–10

Location: full sun, fertile well-drained soil

Growing tip: Many Northerners have seen Lily of the Nile on trips to the South and wished they could grow them. With mulching, deciduous varieties like the 'Headbourne' hybrids are cold hardy to –10F.

Season of performance: summer

Letting the Tiger Loose

'Bengal Tiger' canna stands tall in the garden, capturing attention with its tropical coarse-textured foliage. The yellow and green variegation partners are in harmonic bliss with the spiky violet blue salvias and mass of red coleus. The 'Profusion Orange' zinnia bordering the bed not only complements the 'Victoria Blue' salvia but also helps strengthen the effect of the orange blooms of the canna.

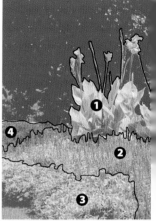

1 'Bengal Tiger' canna (*Canna* x*generalis* 'Bengal Tiger'), zones 7–10

2 'Victoria Blue' mealy-cup sage (*Salvia farinacea* 'Victoria Blue'), zones 7–10

3 'Profusion Orange' zinnia (*Zinnia* 'Profusion Orange'), annual

4 Coleus (*Solenostemon scutellarioides* cv.), annual

Location: full sun, moist fertile well-drained soil

Growing tip: Pinching coleus and cutting back salvias, cannas, and zinnias will rejuvenate plants for an autumn display. Removing old canna stubble will assist with controlling next year's leaf-rolling caterpillars.

Season of performance: summer and autumn

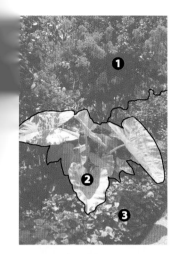

1 'Tonto' crape myrtle
(*Lagerstroemia indica* x *fauriei* 'Tonto'), zones 7–10

2 'Lime Zinger' elephant ear (*Xanthosoma aurea* 'Lime Zinger') zones 7–11

3 Joseph's coat (*Alternanthera ficoidea* cv.), annual

Location: full sun, fertile and well-drained soil

Growing tip: Deadhead crape myrtle to extend the bloom. In colder areas, 'Lime Zinger' bulbs can be dug and stored.

Season of performance: summer and early autumn

Lime Rickey

'Lime Zinger' elephant ear demands attention because of its color and size, both of which scream tropics. Partner it with 'Tonto' red crape myrtle, and you have a giant lime rickey for the landscape. 'Tonto' is accepted as the best red crape myrtle, blooming in excess of 75 days. The Joseph's coat groundcover adds a layer of green lushness to the bed.

Philippine Autumn Fest

The bright yellow and green, tiger-striped foliage of this canna sizzles in the landscape all season, and most gardeners would treasure it even if it never bloomed. It does, however, with intense orange flowers that stand out like lanterns on a post. Once the days get short in autumn, the richly colored flowers of the Philippine violet begin complementing the 'Bengal Tiger', lasting through the first freeze. The maiden grass sways in the wind, creating the feel of being in an island breeze.

1 'Bengal Tiger' canna (*Canna xgeneralis* 'Bengal Tiger'), zones 7–10

2 Philippine violet (*Barleria cristata*), zones 8–11

3 Maiden grass (*Miscanthus sinensis*), zones 4–9

Location: full to part sun, moist fertile well-drained soil, drier conditions and mulch appreciated in the winter

Growing tip: Cut cannas and Philippine violet back to the ground once frozen, and remove stubble from the area.

Season of performance: summer and autumn

Princess Panacea

1 Princess flower
(*Tibouchina urvilleana*),
zones 8–11

**2 'Amazon Rose Magic'
dianthus** (*Dianthus barbatus* interspecific hybrid
'Amazon Rose Magic'),
annual, perennial in zones
6–8b

Location: sun with afternoon shade during summer
heat, well-drained soil rich
with organic matter

Growing tip: Keep
dianthus deadheaded, and
fertilize princess flower
after each bloom cycle.

Season of performance:
late spring through autumn

A royal robe of purple adorns the princess flower, thanks to the scores of vibrantly colored blossoms. This treasured shrubby plant from Brazil deserves a landscape partner that can dazzle but bring harmony to the marriage. Bearing three colors at once, the 'Amazon Rose Magic' dianthus accomplishes this in dramatic fashion. The flowers begin as white, mature to pink, and finish as rose. They are excellent as cut flowers and have an enticing fragrance.

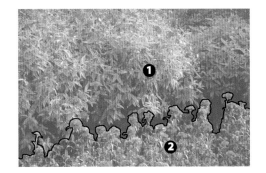

Rajas and Kings

Audiences always gasp in delight at this photo. Incredibly, it could be duplicated in most of the United States with a few simple rules: layer the beds from back to front, and vary the texture. The coarse-textured tropicals 'King Humbert Red' canna, with the bronze foliage, and 'Raja Puri' banana create the illusion of being on an island. The showy variegated eulalia grass gives an entirely different fine-leaf texture, which ties in with the spiky look of the salvia. Toward the front of the bed, there are round umbels from the geranium, variegated foliage from the lantana, and then the fan-shaped flower of the scaevola from Australia. There is a lot to see and admire.

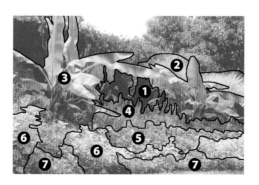

1 'King Humbert Red' canna (*Canna* xgeneralis 'King Humbert Red'), zones 7–11

2 'Variegatus' eulalia grass (*Miscanthus sinensis* 'Variegatus'), zones 5–9

3 'Raja Puri' banana (*Musa* 'Raja Puri'), zones 8–11

4 'Victoria Blue' mealy-cup sage (*Salvia farinacea* 'Victoria Blue'), annual, perennial in zones 7–10

5 Pink geranium (*Pelargonium xhortorum* cv.), annual

6 'Samantha' lantana (*Lantana camara* 'Samantha'), zones (7) 8–10

7 'New Wonder' fan flower (*Scaevola aemula* 'New Wonder'), annual, perennial in zones 9–11

Location: sun, fertile well-drained soil

Growing tip: Deadheading, cutting back, and light applications of fertilizer every 4 to 6 weeks will keep this garden at its best for months.

Season of performance: summer and autumn

Regal Performance

Nothing lends a touch of the tropics to a garden like elephant ears, with their large coarse-textured leaves. In this summer sun garden, the imperial taro partners with the disease-resistant 'Profusion Fire' zinnia to create the illusion that this is South Florida. Because northern gardeners dig up and store imperial taro for the winter, the garden could be grown anywhere. Imperial taro, with its purple black leaves and green veins, makes a nice contrast to the bright orange zinnias.

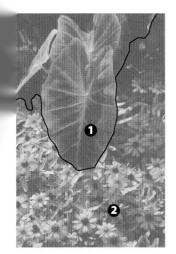

1 'Illustris' imperial taro
(*Colocasia esculenta* 'Illustris'), zones 7–11

2 'Profusion Fire' zinnia
(*Zinnia* 'Profusion Fire'), annual

Location: full to part sun, fertile well-drained soil

Growing tip: In colder areas, dig up the taro bulbs, let the plants dry for a couple of days, remove the foliage, place the bulbs in dry peat, and store in a cool dry place.

Season of performance: late spring through autumn

Royal Princess

This garden may have the ultimate complementary scheme among the tropical gardens, partnering the iridescent purple of the princess flower and the cheerful yellow of the thryallis. The princess flower's leaves, with velvety texture, are often lined in orange, which provides an incredible texture. Many gardeners grow the princess flower as an annual, like they would a tropical hibiscus. In zone 8 it will freeze to the ground and return in spring. Thryallis is a drought-tolerant evergreen shrub from Guatemala and Mexico that reaches 6 feet tall. As temperatures cool, the leaves obtain a unique bronze tone.

1 Princess flower (*Tibouchina urvilleana*), zones 8–11

2 Thryallis (*Galphimia glauca*), zones 8–11

Location: full to part sun, afternoon shade during the hot summer is appreciated, moist fertile well-drained soil

Growing tip: Fertilize the princess flower after each bloom cycle.

Season of performance: summer and autumn

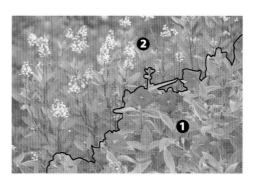

Taste of the Tropics

A banana plant can give an undeniable taste of the tropics no matter where you live. The 'Maurelii' red Abyssinian banana from Africa is considered by many to be the most beautiful banana in the world. It does not sucker, and it is well suited to large pots. The burgundy on the leaves harmonizes with the blossoms of the crape myrtle and the hot pink of the begonias. The dusty miller, with its silver foliage, adds an interesting contrast.

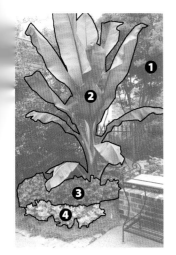

1 'Tonto' crape myrtle (*Lagerstroemia indica* x *fauriei* 'Tonto'), zones 7–10

2 'Maurelii' red Abyssinian banana (*Ensete ventricosum* 'Maurelii'), annual, perennial in zones 9–11

3 'Ambassador Pink' begonia (*Begonia semperflorens* 'Ambassador Pink'), annual

4 Dusty miller (*Senecio cineraria*), annual, perennial in zones 7–10

Location: full to part sun, fertile well-drained soil rich with organic matter

Growing tip: Feed your banana plant regularly during the growing season.

Season of performance: summer through autumn

1 'Bengal Tiger' canna
(*Canna* x*generalis* 'Bengal Tiger'), zones 7–10

2 Coleus (*Solenostemon scutellarioides* cv.), annual

3 Impatiens (*Impatiens walleriana* cv.), annual

4 Joseph's coat (*Alternanthera ficoidea* cv.), annual

Location: morning sun and afternoon shade, well-drained soil rich with organic matter

Growing tip: Joseph's coat can be sheared or cut back to shape it or to maintain its size. Keep flowers pinched on the coleus.

Season of performance: summer and autumn

Tiger Retreat

Flowers have power, but well placed foliage can steal the show. 'Bengal Tiger' canna's foliage forms an idyllic partnership with the smaller leaves of the lime green Joseph's coat displaying the same color. The coleus, which is spot planted, contrasts with its green, cream, and red variegation. The red in the coleus becomes visually stronger thanks to the red impatiens.

Tropical Fiber

This deck will thrive in tropical style all growing season thanks to its daily fiber from the most cold-hardy banana in the world, the Japanese fiber banana. This banana allows gardeners in most parts of the country to add the flavor of the islands to any landscape. Partner it with a ginger and colorful New Guinea impatiens, and you can put on your Hawaiian shirt and let the party begin. The 'SunPatiens' New Guinea impatiens will thrive in full sun.

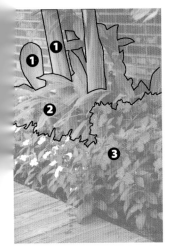

1 Japanese fiber banana (*Musa basjoo*), zones (5) 6–11

2 Shampoo ginger (*Zingiber zerumbet*), zones (7) 8–11

3 'SunPatiens Magenta' and 'SunPatiens White' impatiens (*Impatiens* 'SunPatiens Magenta' and 'SunPatiens White'), annual

Location: full to part sun, fertile well-drained soil rich with organic matter

Growing tip: Feed banana plants regularly, and don't be hesitant to cut back the impatiens as needed.

Season of performance: summer through autumn

Tropical Magic

Boldly textured leaves like these giant elephant ears lend a tropical taste wherever they're grown. Reaching over 6 feet tall, 'Black Magic' and green elephant ears contrast in a striking partnership with their relative, 'Aaron' white caladium. Though smaller, the caladiums show out with many more leaves. The garden also looks patriotic with 'Pacifica Red' periwinkle and 'Blue Daze' evolvulus, which are ruggedly tough.

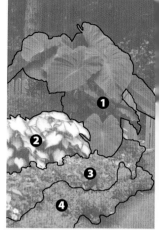

1 'Black Magic' and green type elephant ear (*Colocasia esculenta* 'Black Magic'), annual, perennial in zones 7–11

2 'Aaron' caladium (*Caladium bicolor* 'Aaron'), annual, perennial in zones 10–11

3 'Pacifica Red' Madagascar periwinkle (*Catharanthus roseus* 'Pacifica Red'), annual

4 'Blue Daze' evolvulus (*Evolvulus glomeratus* 'Blue Daze'), annual

Location: full to part sun, fertile well-drained soil rich with organic matter

Growing tip: Good winter drainage is essential for a spring return of elephant ears. In cold regions, bulbs can be dug and stored.

Season of performance: summer and early autumn

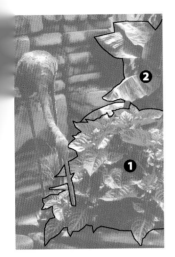

1 'Blazin Rose' iresine
(*Iresine herbstii* 'Blazin Rose'), annual

2 'Sumatrana' bloodleaf banana (*Musa acuminata* 'Sumatrana'), zones 8–11

Location: morning sun and afternoon shade or filtered light, fertile well-drained soil

Growing tip: Tall bananas offer afternoon shade protection for 'Blazin Rose'.

Season of performance: summer through autumn

Tropically Exotic

'Blazin Rose' has proven to be one of the more versatile plants in the filtered-light garden. Native to tropical areas of Brazil and Ecuador, this iresine represents another great choice in colorful foliage for the landscape. At 18 to 30 inches tall and wide, they grow as large as a coleus. In frost-free areas, iresines will grow slightly more as their tropical nature is to reach close to 6 feet tall. Partner with bloodleaf bananas, with their swatches of burgundy in the leaves, and you get a combination that's tropically exotic.

Velvet in Paradise

Lush foliage and pink flowers followed by hot pink velvet-coated fruit make this banana plant a treat for all to grow. In this tropical paradisiacal garden, the banana is combined with the imperial taro and Louisiana iris. Green predominates in the garden, offering a soothing luxuriant atmosphere. The large long leaves of the bananas, broad elephant-ear shapes, and strapped leaves of the iris offer a visually stimulating array of textures as well.

1 Pink velvet banana
(*Musa velutina*), zones 7–11

2 'Illustris' imperial taro
(*Colocasia esculenta* 'Illustris'), annual, perennial in zones 7–11

3 Iris (*Iris* cv.), zones 4–9

Location: part sun, well-drained soil rich with organic matter

Growing tip: Winter drainage is essential for the long-term perennial performance of this garden. Bananas need monthly applications of fertilizer. In colder regions, dig imperial taro bulbs and store.

Season of performance: summer and early autumn

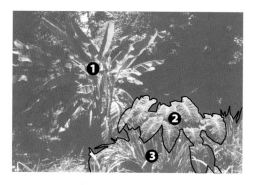

Butterfly and Hummingbird

Whether you call them backyard wildlife habitats, butterfly gardens, or hummingbird gardens, select the right flowers and you'll have it all. It's fun to have hummingbird feeders around the home, but once you start growing flowers for their feeding you'll feel like a proud parent. It's really quite the same when you see a giant swallowtail on a lantana, monarch larvae feeding on milkweed, or a songbird grabbing the seed from a purple coneflower. With the plight of the honeybees, you'll be thrilled by their presence as well. The design possibilities for a butterfly and hummingbird garden are limitless. You are the artistic director of the production, so experiment and have fun.

First, learn about which species of butterflies live in your region of the country and which species of plants they use for nectar and larval food. If you really love butterflies, you need to provide for their larvae, too. Admittedly, caterpillars look like worms and will devour the plants grown as larval food, but you should be just as proud of the monarch caterpillar as you are the butterfly. It's well worth it to be able to watch their graceful flight.

Make the most of your natural setting. Butterflies like edges. Planting low-growing flowers at the edge of a lawn and high flowers at the edges of trees or along a fence is a way to enhance edge habitat. Locate a major part of the garden in a sunny, protected area. Butterflies are cold-blooded and need sun to warm their bodies enough to fly on cool mornings. They also use the sun for orientation. Place flat stones throughout the garden, and you'll see them doing their version of sunbathing. Butterflies appreciate windbreaks. If you have the ability to plant shrubbery to protect the area from the prevailing wind, the butterflies will reward you with an even greater presence.

Most butterflies are wanderers. Ever tried to take a picture of one? They'll stop off temporarily at your garden to partake of food, water, and shelter. When food sources disappear, then it's "Hasta la vista." So plant

flowers with an overlapping bloom period. Plants like lantanas and many salvias bloom from summer through frost. Lantanas, buddleia, butterfly weed, pentas, and salvias are some of the best at attracting both butterflies and hummingbirds.

Because butterfly and hummingbird gardens essentially serve as backyard wildlife habitat, it's important not to use pesticides on any of the plants. Remember that those caterpillars munching away on the 'Silky Gold' bloodflower will someday sprout beautiful wings.

Just like a perennial garden, design your butterfly and hummingbird garden with large drifts of color. Butterflies are attracted to flowers by color, and a large mass is easier to spot. According to some experts, butterflies' favorite color is purple, followed by blue, yellow, white, pink, and orange.

You'll see that the gardens that provide for both can be quite stunning. Both butterflies and hummingbirds are drawn to many of the same flowers, such as 'Flare' hibiscus, 'Graffiti Red Lace' pentas, and flowering tobacco. The cup plant is a favorite as well, and it holds water and provides seeds for birds as well.

1 Narrow leaf sunflower (*Helianthus angustifolius*), zones 6–9

2 Oleander (*Nerium oleander* cv.), zones (7) 8–11

3 Firecracker plant (*Cuphea ignea*), annual, perennial in zones 8–10

4 Cigar flower (*Cuphea micropetala*), annual, perennial in zones 8–10

5 Blue mistflower (*Conoclinium coelestinum*), zones 5–10

6 Mexican petunia (*Ruellia brittoniana*), zones 7–10

7 Lantana (*Lantana camara* cv.), zones (7) 8–10

8 'Snow Nymph' Texas sage (*Salvia coccinea* 'Snow Nymph'), annual, perennial in zones 8–10

9 Yucca (Yucca filamentosa), zones 5–10

10 'Profusion Orange' zinnia (*Zinnia* 'Profusion Orange'), annual

11 'Pink Wave' petunia (*Petunia* 'Pink Wave'), annual

Location: full sun, fertile well-drained soil

Growing tip: Cut back plants as needed to keep in their allotted space.

Season of performance: summer through autumn

Build It and They Will Come

This hummingbird and butterfly garden was a hit. With their tubular flowers, cupheas are simply irresistible to hummingbirds, as is the white-flowered version of the Texas sage. The native blue mistflower, lantana, Mexican petunia, and 'Profusion Orange' zinnia all attract butterflies. The yucca adds a unique texture and spectacular blooms.

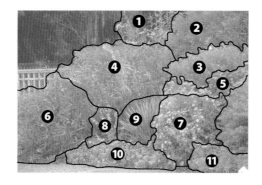

Butterflies and Lace

Gardeners searching for colorful flowers that can take heat and humidity while providing a dazzling display should look no further. These companions partner well for color and heat tolerance, and both attract butterflies. The 'Corona' illuminates the garden with large golden yellow blossoms and a large brown button. It's well branched and compact, reaching 20 inches tall. 'Graffiti Red Lace' is a little shorter, producing deep red flowers well above the foliage, and will attract hummingbirds. The "lace" in the name comes from tiny white filaments protruding from each individual floret.

1 'Graffiti Red Lace' pentas (*Pentas lanceolata* 'Graffiti Red Lace'), annual, perennial in zones 9–11

2 'Corona' rudbeckia (*Rudbeckia hirta* 'Corona'), zones 3–8

Location: full sun, fertile well-drained soil

Growing tip: Pentas like a pH close to 7, so add lime to very acidic soil.

Season of performance: summer

Butterfly and Hummer Heaven

1 Brazilian or anise sage (*Salvia guaranitica*), zones 7–10

2 'Petite Plum' buddleia or butterfly bush (*Buddleja davidii* 'Petite Plum'), zones 5–10

3 'Prairie Sun' and 'Indian Summer' black-eyed Susan (*Rudbeckia hirta* 'Prairie Sun' and 'Indian Summer'), zones 3–10

Location: full to part sun, fertile well-drained soil

Growing tip: Deadheading spent flowers pays dividends with nonstop blooms.

Season of performance: summer and autumn

Plant this garden and children will delight in watching the hummingbirds fight over the iridescent blue flowers of the Brazilian sage. It will be like a National Geographic television special. There will be butterflies, too, not only on the sage but feasting on the 'Petite Plum' buddleia. They don't call buddleia "butterfly bush" for nothing! The blues and plums partner well together and contrast incredibly well with the flashy black-eyed Susans, which will also draw their share of flying visitors.

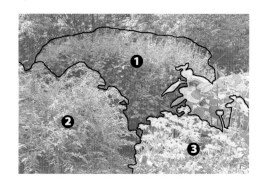

Butterfly Cornucopia

The Cecil B. Day Butterfly Center at Callaway Gardens in Pine Mountain, Georgia, is a must for the young and young at heart. There is nothing quite like walking around in a closed environment as a thousand butterflies flitter around stopping to feed or rest. The grounds outside the conservatory give a glimpse as to what the native butterflies find irresistible. This garden features orange cosmos and an apricot-colored selection of lantana. Butterflies visit both plants, and hummingbirds find the lantanas a delicacy as well.

1 Orange cosmos (*Cosmos sulphureus*), annual

2 Lantana (*Lantana camara* cv.), annual, perennial in zones (7) 8–10

Location: full sun, fertile well-drained soil

Growing tip: Cosmos tolerates poor soil conditions and often reseeds. Fertile soil, good drainage, and added mulch may encourage a spring return for the lantanas in zone 7.

Season of performance: summer through autumn

Butterfly Pye

This garden might not be butterfly heaven, but it's close. 'Gateway' Joe Pye weed is a champion when it comes to providing nectar for the swallowtail butterfly. This selection of the American native is more compact and bushier, producing enormous rose pink flower heads in mid to late summer. Don't let the "weed" in the name fool you, Joe Pye is in the aster family. Here 'Gateway' Joe Pye towers over two more butterfly magnets, 'Indian Summer' black-eyed Susan or gloriosa daisy and 'New Gold' lantana.

1 'Gateway' Joe Pye weed (*Eupatorium maculatum* 'Gateway'), zones 4–9

2 'Indian Summer' black-eyed Susan (*Rudbeckia hirta* 'Indian Summer'), zones 3–8

3 'New Gold' lantana (*Lantana* 'New Gold'), zones (7) 8–10

Location: full sun, fertile well-drained soil

Growing tip: Divide or thin 'Gateway' Joe Pye weed every 3 to 4 years.

Season of performance: summer

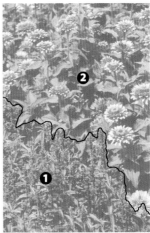

1 'Evolution' mealycup sage (*Salvia farinacea* 'Evolution'), annual, perennial in zones 7–10

2 'Zowie! Yellow Flame' zinnia (*Zinnia violacea* 'Zowie! Yellow Flame'), annual

Location: full sun, fertile well-drained soil

Growing tip: Good winter drainage coupled with a layer of mulch improves the chances for a spring return of the salvia.

Season of performance: summer through autumn

Flaming Evolution

These two plants offer pizzazz and textural interest, and both were selected as All-America Selection winners. They are also both loved by hummingbirds and butterflies. Their opposing colors on the artist wheel, however, make for a marriage of gardening bliss. Over the growing season, the round-flowered zinnias offer multiple colors, starting off a bold magenta pink with yellow tips, and the pink changes to a deep red as the flower matures. The spiky flowers of the salvias offer a totally different texture.

A Flare for Butterflies and Birds

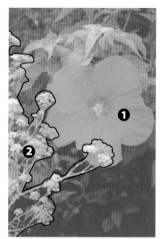

'Flare' hibiscus has become one of the most loved hardy hibiscus available. The fuchsia red blooms almost glow, giving a glimpse into how it received its name. The semi-glossy apple green foliage complements the flowers in striking fashion. 'Flare' has become a staple in the tropical style garden, and those wanting to create a backyard wildlife habitat will also find that it's a delicacy to both hummingbirds and butterflies. The savvy gardener here has partnered it with dill, a great source of larval food for the black swallowtail butterfly. There may be a few jars of pickles, too.

1 'Flare' hardy hibiscus (*Hibiscus moscheutos* 'Flare'), zones 5–10

2 Dill weed (*Anethum graveolens*), annual

Location: full to part sun, fertile soil

Growing tip: Harvest dill when the flowers are open but before seeds have formed.

Season of performance: summer and autumn

Forever Feasting

Hummingbirds and butterflies will be forever feasting tropical style thanks to the bananas and large flowering tobacco, whose white flowers offer tantalizing fragrance and nectar for hummingbirds, butterflies, and sphinx moths. The blue-flowered anise hyssop attracts more bees and butterflies than you can imagine. The Mexican bush sage blooms shortly after the other plants, adding more color and visitors. The lush succulent foliage of the 'Purple Heart' at the front of the border ties everything together.

1 Banana (*Musa* species), zones (7) 8–11

2 Flowering tobacco (*Nicotiana sylvestris*), annual, perennial in zones 10–11

3 Mexican bush sage (*Salvia leucantha*), annual, perennial in zones 7b–10

4 Anise hyssop (*Agastache foeniculum*), annual, perennial in zones 5–9

5 'Purple Heart' setcreasea (*Tradescantia pallida* 'Purple Heart'), annual, perennial in zones 7–10

Location: full sun, fertile well-drained soil

Growing tip: Deadhead old flower stalks of the flowering tobacco for more blooms.

Season of performance: summer through autumn

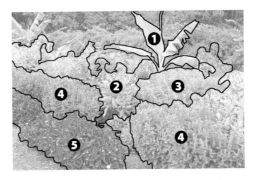

Happy Meal for Hummers

1 Pentas (*Pentas lanceolata* cv.), annual, perennial in zones 9–11

2 'Victoria Blue' mealy-cup sage (*Salvia farinacea* 'Victoria Blue'), annual, perennial in zones 7–10

3 'Profusion Orange' zinnia (*Zinnia* 'Profusion Orange'), annual

Location: full sun, fertile well-drained soil

Growing tip: Pentas like a pH close to 7, so add lime if necessary.

Season of performance: summer and autumn

'Victoria Blue' salvia sends up its spiky blue blossoms all growing season, giving a cottage garden look and creating excitement in the garden by their distinct contrast in the prevailing world of round flowers. Watching hummingbirds, birds, and bees feeding on them and you wonder why everyone doesn't grow these plants. Hummingbirds are even more enamored with the clusters of red star-shaped flowers of the pentas. In addition to attracting butterflies, the 'Profusion Orange' zinnia provides a fiery complement to the blue salvia.

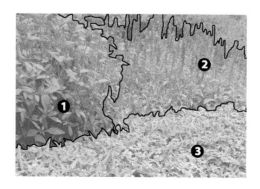

Living Fountain

The cup plant may look like the plant that swallowed Toledo, but this giant can be an integral part of a backyard wildlife habitat. There is nothing this plant can't do. The leaves form a cup that holds water for birds like finches to drink, seeds for the birds to eat, and nectar for butterflies and humming-birds. Our flying friends also treasure the contrasting deep blue flowers of the Brazilian sage. The brown-eyed Susan, although small in comparison, is also a vital native plant for bees and butterflies.

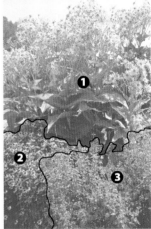

1 Cup plant (*Silphium perfoliatum*), zones 3–9

2 Brown-eyed Susan (*Rudbeckia triloba*), zones 5–9

3 Brazilian or anise sage (*Salvia guaranitica*), zones 7–10

Location: full sun, moist fertile well-drained soil

Growing tip: Let the cup plant create mystery in the garden by blocking a view and forming a transition area.

Season of performance: summer and early autumn

Maid for the Garden

1 'Little Maid' torch lily or red-hot poker (*Kniphofia* 'Little Maid'), zones 6–11

2 'Sunspot' arctotis (*Arctotis* 'Sunspot'), annual, perennial in zones 9–11

3 'Kalipso' euphorbia or spurge (*Euphorbia* 'Kalipso'), zones 6–11

Location: full sun, well-drained soil

Growing tip: These drought-tolerant plants will not like to be overwatered.

Season of performance: summer

This garden ends the notion that drought-tolerant plantings are boring. 'Little Maid' red-hot poker lends an incredible vertical element that breaks the imaginary horizontal plane to create excitement and interest in the garden. Both hummingbirds and butterflies adore it. The lemon yellow and orange spikes partner well with the daisy-like blossoms of the silver-leafed 'Sunspot' arctotis. Because arctotis is still rare in the garden, consider using a rudbeckia as a substitute. 'Kalipso' euphorbia blooms with golden lime or chartreuse flowers from spring through early summer and offers unique foliage texture.

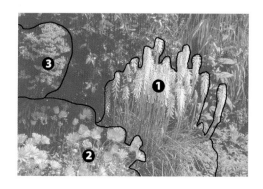

Meadow Magic

National parks like Yosemite or Sequoia no doubt create visions about planting wildflower meadows. Many gardeners have tried to duplicate that at home and probably found little success. If you have only a small area to establish, then a plan using great perennials like the 'Goldsturm' rudbeckia and 'Bravado' purple coneflower could lead you to success. Sprinkle dried seeds from the plants in autumn, do a little dividing every 3 or 4 years, and you will have plenty of butterflies, bees, and birds for years to come.

1 'Goldsturm' black-eyed Susan (*Rudbeckia fulgida* var. *sullivantii* 'Goldsturm'), zones 3–8

2 'Bravado' purple cone-flower (*Echinacea purpurea* 'Bravado'), zones 3–8

Location: full sun, well-drained soil

Growing tip: Young transplants in 4-inch containers without buds are easy to get established.

Season of performance: summer through early autumn

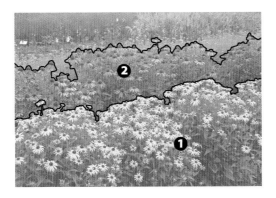

Mexican Fiesta

1 Mexican bush sage
(*Salvia leucantha*), annual,
perennial in zones 7b–10

**2 'Fiesta del Sol' Mexican
sunflower** (*Tithonia
rotundifolia* 'Fiesta del Sol'),
annual

3 'Marvel Gold' and 'Marvel Orange' marigolds
(*Tagetes erecta* 'Marvel
Gold' and 'Marvel Orange'),
annual

Location: full sun, fertile
well-drained soil

Growing tip: Salvias need
good winter drainage and
mulch.

Season of performance:
late summer and autumn

The shorter days of late summer or early autumn bring a Mexican fiesta to gardens with the tall violet-to-purple spikes of the Mexican bush sage. Hummingbirds and butterflies adore the purple, fuzzy, velvet spikes with white flowers. The real fiesta will begin when grown with the annual Mexican sunflower. Though this Mexican native blooms all summer, it really struts its stuff in the autumn, attracting both hummingbirds and butterflies. Cluster 'Marvel Gold' and 'Marvel Orange' African marigolds, and let the fiesta begin.

Monk's Marvel

The lilac chaste tree is really a marvel, with its small structure, large marijuana-looking leaves, and fragrant blue blooms that are rare among trees. The seeds following the blossoms were used medicinally to keep monks' libidos in check, and yet today an extract is made from the seeds to help ladies wanting to get pregnant. In the garden, the flowers attract butterflies and hummingbirds, making this an ideal small tree for the urban backyard wildlife habitat. The tall old-fashioned red pentas likewise attract hummingbirds and butterflies, while giving an added tropical appeal.

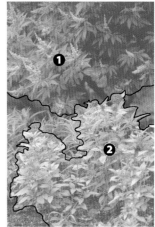

1 Lilac chaste tree (*Vitex agnus-castus*), zones 6–10

2 Pentas (*Pentas lanceolata* cv.), annual, perennial in zones 9–11

Location: full sun, fertile well-drained soil

Growing tip: Many people let *Vitex* grow into a tree, but it can be kept cut back to a shrub and deadheaded to stimulate more blossoms.

Season of performance: summer and autumn

Reflecting on Nectar

1 Joe Pye weed (*Eupatorium maculatum*), zones 4–9

2 Brown-eyed Susan (*Rudbeckia triloba*), zones 5–9

3 Scarlet mallow (*Hibiscus coccineus*), zones 5–10

Location: full to part sun, moist well-drained soil

Growing tip: Place these plants to the back of a border, spacing about 3 feet apart. All of these vigorous perennials may need dividing every 3 or 4 years.

Season of performance: summer and early autumn

This garden is like a resort for butterflies and hummingbirds and no doubt a few bees as well. The rose pink puffy blossoms of the Joe Pye weed offer fragrance and a feast for swallowtail butterflies. These large plants contrast handsomely with the brown-eyed Susan, which is also a nectar source for various butterflies. As tall as the Joe Pye is, it's no match for the scarlet mallow hibiscus, a favorite of both butterflies and hummingbirds.

Silk Stocking Row

Like a silk stocking row, this garden has it all: nectar, larval food, and beauty. Orange and gold dominates in this butterfly garden. While some might think this combination a little overstated, the size of planting was just right and the evergreens provided the perfect backdrop. 'Silky Gold' provides nectar for butterflies and hummingbirds and larval food for monarch butterflies. All of the flowers attract butterflies.

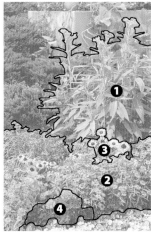

1 'Silky Gold' bloodflower (*Asclepias curassavica* 'Silky Gold'), annual, perennial in zones 8–11

2 'Star Orange' zinnia (*Zinnia angustifolia* 'Star Orange'), annual

3 'Maya' black-eyed Susan (*Rudbeckia hirta* 'Maya'), zones 3–8

4 'Bonanza Flame' marigold (*Tagetes patula* 'Bonanza Flame'), annual

Location: full to part sun, fertile moist well-drained soil

Growing tip: Dried seed pods of the bloodflower can be harvested and used for planting elsewhere.

Season of performance: summer and autumn

You Pickle Me

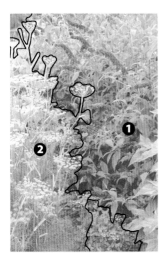

Dill is loved by the culinary artist, the kids who munch giant pickles, and those of us who recognize it as the key ingredient to the hamburger. The leaves of dill weed are also loved by black swallowtail butterfly larvae. The pollen feeds hungry adult lacewings and syrphid flies, two highly beneficial insects to have in the garden. The yellow flowers are also terrific complementary partners for the 'Black Knight' buddleia blooms, which provide food for butterflies.

1 'Black Knight' buddleia or butterfly bush (*Buddleja davidii* 'Black Knight'), zones 5–10

2 Dill weed (*Anethum graveolens*), annual

Location: full to part sun, fertile well-drained soil

Growing tip: Sow successive crops of dill so you'll have plenty for the butterflies and use inside. Let the buddleia grow naturally but do deadhead for more blossoms.

Season of performance: summer and autumn

Grasses

Growing ornamental grasses is a lot easier than you think. A lot of gardeners' fear probably revolves around what to plant with them as companions.
The truth is that you don't have to enroll in design school to learn how to
use ornamental grasses. It is almost as simple as digging a hole, planting
the grass, and tucking in a few of your favorite blooming flowers. Also, you
don't have to have massive expanses of grass. Sure, that can be thrilling,
but never underestimate the power of one small grass with its colorful fine
leaf texture.

Blooming ornamental grasses add a new dimension to the landscape.
Like vines, grasses add a vertical element, but grasses do something few
people think about—they move. As its name suggest, the 'Wind Dancer'
love grass performs a ballet in the wind that no choreographer could duplicate. Back and forth it sways as the wind dictates: slow and gentle or fast
and swirling. 'Wind Dancer' is not alone, muhly grass, resembling a large
cloud of hot pink cotton candy, can hold you in a mesmerizing stare.

Grasses do something else that is incredible: they glisten like they have
a coat of ice when backlit by the setting sun or landscape lighting. Speak-
ing of ice, the frosty kiss of those cold autumn mornings makes ornamental grasses the prettiest plants in the landscape. In the dead of winter, a
Mexican feather grass with not a hint of green looks as picturesque as a
piece of statuary when lighted at night.

Before planting ornamental grasses, it is critical to remove unwanted
vegetation. Many disgruntled gardeners have found that aggressive Ber-
muda grass or vines make themselves at home intermingled with ornamental grasses. Similar to planting a perennial or small shrub, set nurs-
ery-grown transplants in loose, well-prepared, organic-rich beds. Plant at
the same depth they are growing in the container, placing the crown of
the plant slightly above the soil line. Water thoroughly and add a layer of
mulch.

Ballet in the Landscape

'Wind Dancer', a selection of native love grass, lives up to its name when in bloom. It sways and dances back and forth in more than one direction at a time, adding the dimension of motion to the garden. The plumes mature to a tan color in August and a lighter straw color in autumn, maintaining winter interest. Here it makes a striking contrast in texture and color with 'Landmark Peach Sunrise' lantana.

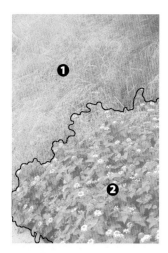

1 'Wind Dancer' love grass (*Eragrostis elliottii* 'Wind Dancer'), zones 6–10

2 'Landmark Peach Sunrise' lantana (*Lantana camara* 'Landmark Peach Sunrise'), zones (7) 8–10

Location: full sun, fertile well-drained soil

Growing tip: Pruning the lantana during the growing season will stimulate more growth and blooms. Using three to five 'Wind Dancer' in clusters to separate other perennials is very striking.

Season of performance: summer and autumn

Color with a Twist

It's rare when grass offers complementary color in the garden, but that's the role 'Toffee Twist' sedge plays with the 'Blue Bird' nemesia. 'Toffee Twist' reaches about 18 inches in height before spilling over and offers a much-appreciated fine leaf texture. 'Blue Bird' nemesia is planted in the same season as its relative the snapdragon (autumn in the South or spring in the North). 'Blue Bird' has an equally complementary marriage with the blooms of 'Sunny Dark Florence'.

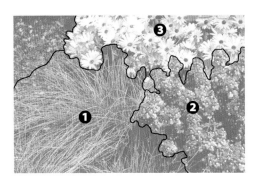

1 'Toffee Twist' sedge (*Carex flagellifera* 'Toffee Twist'), annual, perennial in zones 7–11

2 'Blue Bird' nemesia (*Nemesia* 'Blue Bird'), annual

3 'Sunny Dark Florence' osteospermum (*Osteospermum* 'Sunny Dark Florence'), annual, perennial in zones 9–11

Location: full to part sun, fertile well-drained soil

Growing tip: For a similar combination that performs in summer, plant summer snapdragons such as *Angelonia angustifolia* 'Serena Purple' in place of the nemesia and black-eyed Susan (*Rudbeckia hirta*) in place of the osteospermum.

Season of performance: spring

Cosmic Bunny

1 'Little Bunny' fountain grass (*Pennisetum alopecuroides* 'Little Bunny'), zones 5–10

2 Sulfur cosmos (*Cosmos sulphureus* cv.), annual

3 'Tilt-a-whirl' coleus (*Solenostemon scutellarioides* 'Tilt-a-Whirl'), annual

Location: full to part sun, fertile well-drained soil

Growing tip: Keep flower buds pinched off the coleus to keep new leaves coming. Prior to growth in the spring cut the grass back to 6 or 8 inches.

Season of performance: summer through autumn

Coleus and grasses aren't your typical companions but everything about this garden caught my eye. The reflective white flowers of the 'Little Bunny' are glistening contrasts to the darker rusty red leaves of the coleus with the unusual twist in its structure. The white flowers however are in perfect harmony with the old broken container serving as a decorative accent. The spot color from the yellow cosmos is just enough to draw your attention without overpowering the garden.

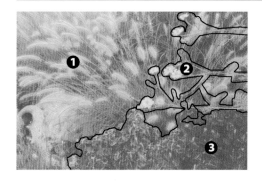

Cotton Candy for the Garden

Blooms resembling pink cotton candy thrill all who grow muhly grass. Blooming in late summer through autumn, muhly grass partners with an array of flowers and embellishes the perennial, cottage, or rose garden. Here the design is simple: dwarf pampas with white plumes contrast with the muhly, and 'Livin' Easy' floribunda rose offers harmony in color but a different texture. Although the muhly is just green structure during most of the summer, the pampas grass and the rose offer continuous bloom.

1 Pink muhly grass (*Muhlenbergia capillaris*), zones 5–9

2 'Pumila' dwarf pampas grass (*Cortaderia selloana* 'Pumila'), zones 5–10

3 'Livin' Easy' floribunda rose (*Rosa* 'Livin' Easy'), zones 5–10

Location: full sun, fertile well-drained soil

Growing tip: For a dazzling rose bloom that coincides with the muhly, prune 'Livin' Easy' by one-third in early August.

Season of performance: late summer and autumn

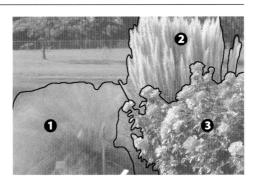

Danish in the Garden

'Karl Foerster' feather reed grass was imported to the United States from Denmark in 1964, and it was selected as the Perennial Plant of the Year by the Perennial Plant Association. This ornamental grass reaches 3 to 5 feet tall. Its light pink feathery plumes appear in early summer and turn golden tan as they mature. Here in late summer, the plumes contrast well with the large rose-colored blooms of the 'Gateway' Joe Pye weed and the pink turtlehead loaded with showy pink blooms.

1 'Karl Foerster' feather reed grass (*Calamagrostis xacutiflora* 'Karl Foerster'), zones 4–9

2 'Gateway' Joe Pye weed (*Eupatorium maculatum* 'Gateway'), zones 4–9

3 Pink turtlehead (*Chelone obliqua*), zones 4–8

Location: full sun, fertile moist well-drained soil

Growing tip: 'Karl Foerster' blooms are often striking in winter, but these should be cut back before spring growth.

Season of performance: summer and autumn

Photo courtesy of the Perennial Plant Association

Electric Grass

Fiber optic grass is among the hottest plants for the landscape. The grass forms mounds of thin blades with small rounded blooms on the tips. They are indeed reminiscent of fiber optic filaments, giving the idea you might flip a switch and turn the plant on. The deep green color means it will combine with just about any partner imaginable. The bright golden chartreuse 'Sweet Kate' makes a stunning marriage of leaf textures and color.

1 Fiber optic grass
(*Isolepis cernua*), annual, perennial in zones 8–11

2 'Sweet Kate' spiderwort
(*Tradescantia* 'Sweet Kate'), zones 4–11

Location: full to part sun, moist fertile well-drained soil

Growing tip: Another outstanding companion for fiber optic grass is coleus. 'Sweet Kate' and fiber optic grass also excel in containers.

Season of performance: summer through autumn

1 'King Tut' papyrus
(*Cyperus papyrus* 'King Tut'),
annual, perennial in zones
8–11

**2 'High Tide Blue' agera-
tum** (*Ageratum housto-
nianum* 'High Tide Blue'),
annual

Location: full to part sun,
fertile soil

Growing tip: Papyrus
selections are well suited
for water gardens. It's a
good idea to simply grow
the plants in a sunken container, which manages their
spread and lets you easily
move them for cold protection and maintenance.

Season of performance:
summer and autumn

Fit for a King

The clear pool and blue ageratums make a nice partnership. But add 'King
Tut' papyrus, and you create a picturesque poolside garden enticing you
to go for a dip on a warm summer day. 'King Tut', a dwarf variety of the
regular Egyptian papyrus, gracefully arches over, giving a tufted or hairy
appearance with its umbrellas. The reed-like stems give the landscape a
lush tropical feel.

Her Majesty's Service

'Purple Majesty' draws the eye to this garden, with its dark purple foliage and almost black blooms. It serves as a foil for the 'High Tide Blue' ageratum. More drifts of color are provided by 'Madness Salmon Morn' petunia, 'Serena White' angelonia, and 'Rising Sun' coreopsis, all playing off the dark's purple leaves of 'Purple Majesty'. The banana plant's lighter green and large leaves provide a good counterpoint to the dark narrow leaves of the millet.

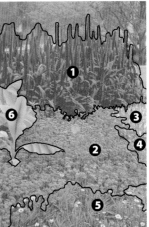

1 'Purple Majesty' ornamental millet (*Pennisetum glaucum* 'Purple Majesty'), annual

2 'High Tide Blue' ageratum (*Ageratum houstonianum* 'High Tide Blue'), annual

3 'Serena White' angelonia (*Angelonia angustifolia* 'Serena White'), annual

4 'Madness Salmon Morn' petunia (*Petunia* 'Madness Salmon Morn'), annual

5 'Rising Sun' coreopsis (*Coreopsis grandiflora* 'Rising Sun'), zones 4–9

6 Japanese fiber banana (*Musa basjoo*), zones (5) 6–11

Location: full sun, fertile well-drained soil

Growing tip: Set transplants of 'Purple Majesty' while they are young and not root bound.

Season of performance: spring and summer

Holy Mowly

St. Augustine grass is a favorite turf in the southern regions of the United States, and the variegated variety may prove to be the showy groundcover for which many have been searching. The creamy white and green variegation is a bright contrast with the broad dark leaves of 'Red Flash' caladium. Variegated St. Augustine is not used as a turf grass but excels in containers, where it can fall over the edge, or as a small groundcover that produces a sea of white.

1 'Red Flash' caladium
(*Caladium bicolor* 'Red Flash'), annual, perennial in zones 10–11

2 Variegated St. Augustine grass (*Stenotaphrum secundatum* var. *variegatum*), annual, perennial in zones 8–11

Location: morning sun and afternoon shade, fertile well-drained soil rich with organic matter

Growing tip: Though this ornamental grass can be mowed, hand thinning and keeping the plants slightly tall give the best look.

Season of performance: summer and autumn

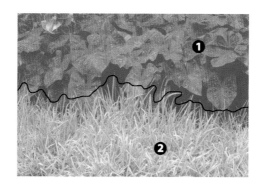

Plethora of Plumes

This combination has a plethora of plumes, from the purple fountain grass to the contrasting white blooms of the dwarf pampas grass. The yellow spikes of the forsythia sage begin to bloom in autumn and serve as a final delicacy for the ruby-throated hummingbirds beginning their trek southward. Purple fountain grass works in harmony with the red tones in the salmon and coral zinnias.

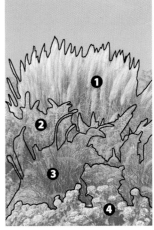

1 'Pumila' dwarf pampas grass (*Cortaderia selloana* 'Pumila'), zones 5–10

2 Forsythia sage (*Salvia madrensis*), zones 7–10

3 Purple fountain grass (*Pennisetum setaceum*), annual, perennial in zones 9–11

4 'Magellan Coral' and 'Magellan Salmon' zinnias (*Zinnia violacea* 'Magellan Coral' and 'Magellan Salmon'), annual

Location: full sun, fertile well-drained soil

Growing tip: Forsythia sage blooms under long night or short day conditions so don't plant under streetlights.

Season of performance: summer and autumn

Pluminous Garden

Cross the word *luminous* with *plumes* and you get *pluminous*, which i[s] just what you have in this backlit garden. The foxtail blooms of the purple fountain grass glow and contrast beautifully with its dark foliage and the iridescent blue flowers of the Mexican petunia. The leaf color of the purple fountain grass works in monochromatic harmony with the Mexican petunia stems. The 'Marguerite' sweet potato vine's bright chartreuse foliage makes a great complement with the petunia's blue flowers.

1 Purple fountain grass (*Pennisetum setaceum*), annual, perennial in zones 9–11

2 Mexican petunia (*Ruellia brittoniana*), annual, perennial in zones 7–10

3 'Marguerite' ornamental sweet potato (*Ipomoea batatas* 'Marguerite'), annual

Location: full sun, fertile well-drained soil

Growing tip: Tight heavy soil prevents the Mexican petunia from reaching its potential. Under good conditions, though, watch for unwanted volunteers.

Season of performance: summer and autumn

Purple Panache

The foxtail plumes of the purple fountain grass contrast glowingly against the backdrop of green shrubbery and partner harmoniously with the purple foliage of the canna and blooms of Mexican petunia. The spiky blue flowers of the salvia complement the brilliant blooms of the 'New Gold' lantana.

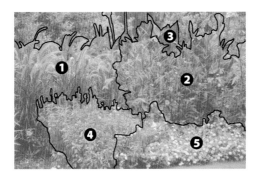

1 Purple fountain grass (*Pennisetum setaceum*), annual, perennial in zones 9–11

2 Mexican petunia (*Ruellia brittoniana*), annual, perennial in zones 7–10

3 'Wyoming' canna (*Canna* x*generalis* 'Wyoming'), zones 7–10

4 'Victoria Blue' mealy-cup sage (*Salvia farinacea* 'Victoria Blue'), annual, perennial in zones 7–10

5 'New Gold' lantana (*Lantana camara* 'New Gold'), annual, perennial in zones (7) 8–10

Location: full sun, fertile well-drained soil

Growing tip: Cut salvias and lantanas back as needed in late summer to regenerate growth and blooms.

Season of performance: summer and autumn

Senorita Bronzita

1 'Bronzita' carex (*Carex flagellifera* 'Bronzita'), zones 7–11

2 'Fresh Look Yellow' celosia (*Celosia argentea* 'Fresh Look Yellow'), annual

3 'Star Orange' zinnia (*Zinnia angustifolia* 'Star Orange'), annual

Location: full sun, fertile well-drained soil

Growing tip: These plants are all drought tolerant and tough, but provide a little supplemental water during prolonged dryness to keep the plants looking their best.

Season of performance: summer and autumn

With its unique coppery color, 'Bronzita' gives a look to the garden like few other grasses—or in this case, a sedge—can do. The plant's habit is also picturesque, as it grows upward 15 to 18 inches and then gently curves downward. The fine leaf texture of 'Bronzita' stands out, giving a remarkable contrast with the neighboring round-flowered zinnias and spiky blooms of the celosias. The copper, oranges, and yellows all partner in harmony.

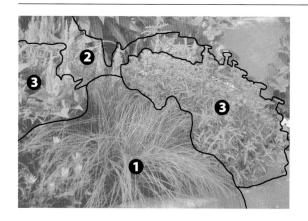

Streets of Gold

Golden miniature sweet flag winds its way around a cluster of 'Nikko Blue' hydrangeas, giving the illusion of a street of gold. Like giant blue sapphires, the hydrangeas complement the golden lime foliage of this very dwarf grass-like plant. Golden miniature sweet flag reaches around 3 inches in height before gently curving toward the ground. It's tolerant of a lot of soil conditions including exceedingly moist soils, but this is not so with the hydrangea.

1 'Nikko Blue' hydrangea (*Hydrangea macrophylla* 'Nikko Blue'), zones (5) 6–9

2 'Minimus Aureus' golden miniature sweet flag (*Acorus gramineus* 'Minimus Aureus'), zones 5–8

Location: filtered light or morning sun and afternoon shade, fertile soil

Growing tip: Should sweet flag foliage get unattractive, cut back in late winter before the new spring growth. Sweet flag can spread over the years, so divide as needed.

Season of performance: summer

24-Karat Gold

'Victoria Blue' salvia provides a cottage garden look and a complementary partner for the 'Evergold' sedge, a fine-textured element. Never underestimate the power of a well-placed golden leafed grass like 'Evergold'. Add 'Intensia Neon Pink' phlox to the mix and the garden turns into a blissful triadic harmony. The 'Diamond Frost' euphorbia serves as a glistening white accent that's virtually indestructible in the summer landscape.

1 'Victoria Blue' mealy-cup sage (*Salvia farinacea* 'Victoria Blue'), annual, perennial in zones 7–10

2 'Intensia Neon Pink' phlox (*Phlox* 'Intensia Neon Pink'), annual, perennial in zones 9–11

3 'Evergold' sedge (*Carex hangzhouensis* 'Evergold'), zones 5–9

4 'Diamond Frost' euphorbia (*Euphorbia* 'Diamond Frost'), annual, perennial in zones 9–11

Location: full sun, fertile well-drained soil

Growing tip: Cut back phlox and salvia in late summer to encourage new blooms for autumn.

Season of performance: late spring through autumn

Foliage and Flower

Never underestimate the power of foliage in the landscape. Whether you grow foliage with more foliage or foliage with flowers, incorporating plants like coleus, sweet potatoes, Joseph's coat, duranta, and countless others will transform your landscape into a real garden. Foliage plants like the ornamental sweet potatoes can fill in space very quickly, giving gardeners great value for the dollars spent. With this quick spread they can be used as groundcovers, allowed to drape over walls, and used as a vertical element plummeting downward from baskets or containers.

Foliage plants also have a tremendously long duration of performance, acting as the workhorses in the garden as perennials and annuals come and go within their respective seasons. Incredibly, they usually do all of this with little insect or disease pressure, only asking for fertile well-drained soil and maybe a little pinching every now and then.

As you study these combinations, notice that in many instances the foliage is striking but it also enhances or intensifies the color of the adjacent flowers. Such is the ability of the 'Purple Knight' alternanthera, with its dark purple leaves, or the 'Black Pearl' ornamental pepper, which is so dark it's barely distinguishable from black. Incorporate several plants that stand out because of their foliage, and you'll have a garden that looks good all season long.

Use foliage in combination with flowers in color schemes that are complementary or slightly more sophisticated, as well as in sun or shade. Foliage can also be used to echo the color of the flowers. Notice how caladiums can reflect the colors of impatiens or how coleus echoes begonias. Then there is a special group of plants including canna, toad lily, and yucca that not only offer colorful foliage but also blooms that can be considered among the most picturesque in the garden world.

Alluring Glow

Most of us first encountered the word *fusion* in physics or chemistry class, but now it's one of the hottest new impatiens varieties. The Fusion series produces flowers that resemble seashells with bicolored centers. In addition to the exotic shape, the colors are also unique. They'll show out in your landscape from the day you plant them until the first frost, so it's wise to have a partner that also has staying power, like this 'Aurora Black Cherry' coleus. The darker leaves with green margins accentuate the colorful impatiens.

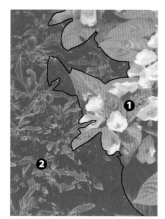

1 'Fusion Glow Improved' impatiens (*Impatiens balsamina* 'Fusion Glow Improved'), annual

2 'Aurora Black Cherry' coleus (*Solenostemon scutellarioides* 'Aurora Black Cherry'), annual

Location: filtered sun or morning sun and afternoon shade, fertile soil rich with organic matter

Growing tip: In late summer, trim back coleus and impatiens about one-third to induce branching and new growth.

Season of performance: summer through autumn

An Artist's Touch

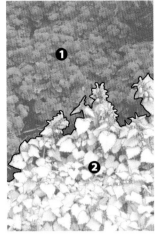

'Artist Purple' has been capturing honors across the country, and it will steal your heart as well. The rare color that might be considered magenta or even maroon is much sought after in the world of flowers. In this alluring display, it's partnered with 'Pink Chablis' lamium. Even if 'Pink Chablis' never bloomed, its showy variegated foliage of white or silver would highlight or complement the dark purple magenta flowers of the ageratum, making them even richer in color. The lamium does send up spikes of pink flowers, strengthening the marriage.

1 'Artist Purple' ageratum
(*Ageratum* 'Artist Purple'),
annual

2 'Pink Chablis' lamium
(*Lamium maculatum* 'Pink Chablis'), zones 4–9

Location: full to part sun, fertile well-drained soil

Growing tip: Lamium is shade tolerant and needs more moisture in summer's sunnier locations.

Season of performance:
late spring through early autumn

As Pretty as a Flower

These plants are called flowering kale, but it's the leaves that are as pretty as a flower. Though not edible, the leaves do make an artistic garnish for your culinary endeavors. In this landscape the red and white kale echo the colors found on the ever-changing 'Amazon Rose Magic' dianthus, whose flowers begin as white, mature to pink, and finish as rose. They are excellent as cut flowers and have an enticing fragrance.

1 'Amazon Rose Magic' dianthus (*Dianthus barbatus* interspecific hybrid 'Amazon Rose Magic'), annual, perennial in zones 6–8b

2 'Chidori Red' and 'Chidori White' flowering kale (*Brassica oleracea* 'Chidori Red' and 'Chidori White'), annual

Location: full sun, fertile well-drained soil rich with organic matter

Growing tip: Flowering kale is very cold hardy but can be covered for a few days with a blanket of pine straw if needed.

Season of performance: autumn though spring

Black and White

Never has a pepper garnered so much admiration as has the 'Black Pearl'. Even if the plants did not bloom or set fruit, you would welcome them into the garden for their foliage, which is so deep purple it's nearly black. 'Black Pearl' does produce a bounty of marble-sized, shiny black peppers that mature to glistening red. While the fruits are showy, it's the leaves that most rave about because they partner with just about any combination imaginable. Here the companion is the contrasting white of the drought-tolerant, ruggedly tough 'Tequila Cream' moss rose or portulaca.

1 'Black Pearl' pepper (*Capsicum annuum* 'Black Pearl'), annual

2 'Tequila Cream' portulaca (*Portulaca grandiflora* 'Tequila Cream'), annual

Location: full sun, fertile well-drained soil

Growing tip: Feed your peppers every 3 to 4 weeks with a 1–2–1 fertilizer.

Season of performance: summer

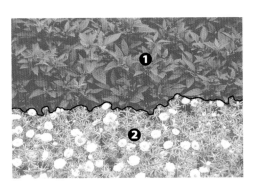

Carpet of Gold

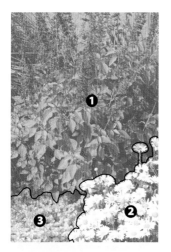

'Goldilocks' lysimachia forms a ground-hugging carpet of gold or char
treuse, garnering attention no matter what companion planting you use
Here it really enhances its partners' floral displays. This garden is packed
with interest, with the tall violet blue spikes of the 'Indigo Spires' creating
excitement and contrasting with the lime green disk-shaped leaves of 'Gol
dilocks' and the pristine white Nippon daisies. Both the salvias and the dai
sies attract butterflies as well.

1 'Indigo Spires' salvia
(*Salvia* 'Indigo Spires'),
annual, perennial in zones
7–11

**2 Montauk or Nippon
daisy** (*Nipponanthemum
nipponicum*), zones 5–9

3 'Goldilocks' lysimachia
(*Lysimachia nummularia*
'Goldilocks'), zones 3–11

Location: full sun, fertile
moist well-drained soil rich
with organic matter

Growing tip: Cut the
perennial daisies back by
half in late spring to stimulate better branching.

Season of performance:
midsummer through
autumn

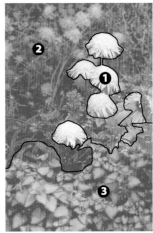

1 'Ice Star' Shasta daisy
(*Leucanthemum* x*superbum* 'Ice Star'), zones 4–10

2 'Harlequin Blue' scabiosa (*Scabiosa columbaria* 'Harlequin Blue'), zones 5–9

3 'Beacon Silver' lamium (*Lamium maculatum* 'Beacon Silver'), zones 4–9

Location: full to part sun, fertile well-drained soil

Growing tip: 'Beacon Silver' appreciates some afternoon shade in hotter climates.

Season of performance: late spring and summer

Coconut Topping

Everyone loves Shasta daisies, but when they look like shredded coconut on cupcakes, all you can say is "Wow." The 'Ice Star' Shasta's lavender blue partner, 'Harlequin Blue' scabiosa, is certainly no slouch either, producing blossoms that are among the most intricate in structure. Gardeners are beginning to use 'Beacon Silver' lamium, with its showy variegated silver leaves with green margins, as a groundcover. Add light purple flowers, and you have a great combination.

Cool-Season Bouquet

1 'Peacock', 'Pigeon', 'Chidori', 'Kamome', and 'Coral' kale (*Brassica oleracea*), annual

2 'Palette' snapdragon (*Antirrhinum majus* 'Palette'), annual

3 'Telstar' dianthus (*Dianthus barbatus* x *chinensis* 'Telstar'), annual, perennial in zones 6–9

4 'Nature' pansy (*Viola* x*wittrockiana* 'Nature'), annual

Location: full sun, fertile soil rich with organic matter

Growing tip: Feed with dilute water-soluble fertilizer every 2 to 3 weeks.

Season of performance: late autumn through spring in the South, spring and early summer in the North

This spring landscape bouquet defies all textbook instruction, challenges our comfort zone, and stretches our design technique. It is the randomness of this combination that makes it work. Randomly plant kale varieties, spacing them 12 to 18 inches apart. In between plant a snapdragon here, a pansy there, a dianthus in the next vacant spot. Repeat this process until the bed is full.

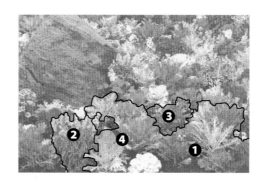

Crimson Blaze

Your shady retreat can be a blaze of color and texture with a trio like the taller 'Blazin Rose' iresine, the spreading 'Fanfare Bight Coral' impatiens, and the compact 'Aurora Black Cherry' coleus. 'Blazin Rose' iresine has the ability to work with other shades of red—whether it's a coral or a hot pink partner—like very few plants can do. This planting requires part shade to filtered light as 'Blazin Rose' can and will scorch in hot afternoon sun.

1 'Fanfare Bright Coral' impatiens (Impatiens 'Fanfare Bright Coral'), annual

2 'Blazin Rose' iresine (*Iresine herbstii* 'Blazin Rose'), annual

3 'Aurora Black Cherry' coleus (*Solenostemon scutellarioides* 'Aurora Black Cherry'), annual

Location: filtered sun, fertile well-drained soil

Growing tip: Feed 'Blazin Rose' with frequent light applications of fertilizer.

Season of performance: late spring through autumn

Dragon Meets Kong

The bright lime green of the 'Kong Red' coleus lights up the shade garden. Among the largest of any coleus, 'Kong Red' leaves also have burgundy and a fiery red that's similar to the shade in the 'Dragon Wing Red' begonia. 'Dragon Wing Red' is lush, vigorous, and able to grow in sun or shade. The deep green leaves of 'Mona Lavender' have purple undersides and serve as a perfect backdrop. This plectranthus will add to the show when it starts sending up its light lavender spikes.

1 'Mona Lavender' plectranthus (*Plectranthus* 'Mona Lavender'), annual, perennial in zones 10–11

2 'Kong Red' coleus (*Solenostemon scutellariodies* 'Kong Red'), annual

3 'Dragon Wing Red' begonia (*Begonia* 'Dragon Wing Red'), annual, perennial in zones 10–11

Location: shade or filtered light, fertile moist soil rich with organic matter

Growing tip: Keep flower buds pinched on the coleus, and cut back the begonia as needed.

Season of performance: summer through early autumn

1 'Electric Lime' coleus
(*Solenostemon scutellarioides* 'Electric Lime'), annual

2 'SunPatiens Orange' impatiens (*Impatiens* 'SunPatiens Orange'), annual

3 'Titan Blue Halo' vinca
(*Catharanthus roseus* 'Titan Blue Halo'), annual

4 'Gold Mound' duranta
(*Duranta erecta* 'Gold Mound'), annual, perennial in zones 9–11

Location: full to part sun, fertile well-drained soil

Growing tip: These plants are all vigorous, so space them to allow enough room to grow and show.

Season of performance: spring through autumn

Electrically Charged

'Electric Lime' coleus will add some voltage to your garden. This cultivar will perform anywhere you plant it. In this entryway flowerbed, 'Electric Lime' has reached close to 3 feet tall and is combined with 'SunPatiens Orange', a New Guinea impatiens hybrid. This variety can take full sun and actually thrive. 'Titan Blue Halo' vinca partners well with the impatiens, and the 'Gold Mound' carries on the chartreuse for a stunning display.

Emperor's Rainbow

Although coleus are native to Africa and Malaysia, in your garden they'll provide foliage as colorful as carnival time in Rio. The shade garden literally explodes with color thanks to varieties like 'Superfine Rainbows Color Pride'. In the shade garden, coleus partner well with flowering plants like impatiens and 'Emperor Rose' begonia. No longer does the shade or filtered-light garden have to go unnoticed, with dark green being the predominant color.

1 'Superfine Rainbows Color Pride' coleus (*Solenostemon scutellarioides* 'Superfine Rainbows Color Pride'), annual

2 'Emperor Rose' begonia (*Begonia semperflorens* 'Emperor Rose'), annual

Location: shade to filtered light, fertile well-drained soil rich with organic matter

Growing tip: We grow coleus for the vibrant colorful foliage, so there's no reason to let the flowers develop. Keep the flowers pinched off and plants fed to keep the leaves coming.

Season of performance: summer through autumn

Kissing the Toad

It would be hard to create a woodland garden with any more appeal than what you have with these companions. The toad lily, with its long arching foliage with hints of chartreuse, complements the maturing blossoms of the hydrangea. The blossoms started off creamy white earlier in the growing season and are now maturing to deep rose. The toad lily also produces showy blossoms in late summer and autumn.

1 Panicle hydrangea (*Hydrangea paniculata* cv.), zones 3–8

2 Toad lily (*Tricyrtis* sp.), zones 4–9

Location: filtered light of a woodland garden, moist fertile soil rich with organic matter

Growing tip: Toad lily also combines well with ferns and hostas. Let toad lily naturalize, and pay attention to water during prolonged dry periods.

Season of performance: summer through autumn

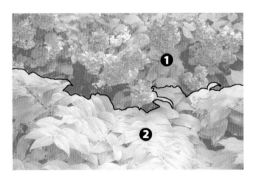

Mystifying Garden Pleasure

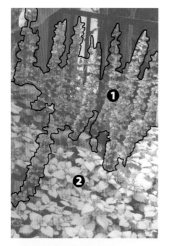

'Mystic Spires Blue', the first compact selection of 'Indigo Spires', is the ideal spiky plant for cottage or perennial gardens. The combination with 'Beacon Silver' lamium is not one you'll soon forget. The silver leaves with green margins highlight the tall intense blue flowers. During much of the growing season 'Beacon Silver' is adorned with pinkish purple flowers, giving a more colorful look to the partnership.

1 'Mystic Spires Blue' salvia (*Salvia* 'Mystic Spires Blue'), annual, perennial in zones 7–11

2 'Beacon Silver' lamium (*Lamium maculatum* 'Beacon Silver'), zones 3–9

Location: full to part sun, fertile well-drained soil

Growing tip: 'Mystic Spires Blue' fits perfectly in the backyard wildlife habitat, attracting butterflies, bees, and hummingbirds. Salvias need good drainage even more so in the winter.

Season of performance: summer through autumn

Rubies for the Queen

This is a great combination for those gardeners who are frantic to find color for the shade. By combining with impatiens, fancy-leafed caladiums like 'White Queen' offer unique possibilities for the shade garden. The design is simple: Pick out caladiums with a strong multicolored leaf, and use impatiens that have a similar color. In this garden, the 'White Queen' caladiums have pronounced red veins. The 'Super Elfin Ruby' is an ideal match. As the sun sets in the evening, the red colors retreat but the white of the caladiums remains.

1 'White Queen' caladium (*Caladium bicolor* 'White Queen'), annual, perennial in zones 10–11

2 'Super Elfin Ruby' impatiens (*Impatiens walleriana* 'Super Elfin Ruby'), annual

Location: shade or filtered light, fertile moist soil rich with organic matter

Growing tip: The caladiums can be dug and stored in dry peat for the winter.

Season of performance: summer through early autumn

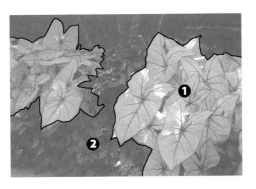

Silver Shadows

1 'Beacon Silver' lamium (*Lamium maculatum* 'Beacon Silver'), zones 3–9

2 'Silver Mound' artemisia (*Artemisia schmidtiana* 'Silver Mound'), zones 3–8

3 'Wildfire Violet' verbena (*Verbena* 'Wildfire Violet'), zones 6–10

Location: full sun, well-drained soil

Growing tip: Cutting back plays an important role in maintaining the look and performance of this planting.

Season of performance: spring through autumn

In a gardening world dominated by a sea of green, well-placed pockets of plants with silver and gray leaves are ever so striking. Here 'Beacon Silver' lamium and 'Silver Mound' artemisia intensify the magenta of the 'Wildfire Violet' verbena. Though we think of artemisia as an herb, it's definitely at home in this perennial garden. Although this beautiful combination looks delicate, in fact these plants are drought tolerant and ruggedly tough.

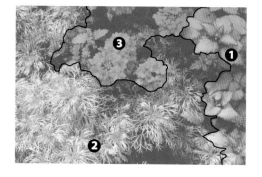

Sunny Side Up

Orange reaches out and grabs your attention. This may be just what you want if you only have a small area for flowers. Orange naturally works with its golden, yellow, and red neighbors. The marigolds, zinnias, and gazanias grow 10 to 15 inches in height, but this walled garden will have a larger vertical appeal thanks to the 'Goldilocks' lysimachia. Though only gently spilling over the wall now, it will literally plummet later in the season.

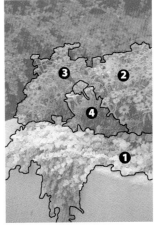

1 'Goldilocks' lysimachia
(*Lysimachia nummularia* 'Goldilocks'), zones 3–11

2 'Star Orange' zinnia
(*Zinnia angustifolia* 'Star Orange'), annual

3 'Durango Flame' marigold (*Tagetes patula* 'Durango Flame'), annual

4 'Daybreak Red Stripe' gazania (*Gazania* 'Daybreak Red Stripe'), annual, perennial in zones 8–11

Location: full sun, fertile well-drained soil

Growing tip: 'Goldilocks' makes an exceptional plant for baskets and planters or anywhere a vertical element is needed.

Season of performance: summer through autumn

Thread of Gold

'Sweet Caroline Sweetheart Lime Green' ornamental sweet potato winds its way like a thread of gold through the jewel-like Cathedral salvias. The plants in this combination are both vigorous and tough. The spiky salvia flowers are loved by both hummingbirds and butterflies. They create excitement as they rise up above the lime green foliage of their companion. The Sweet Caroline series of sweet potatoes now boasts nine distinct leaf shapes or colors for the garden.

**1 'Cathedral Deep Blue',
'Cathedral Sky Blue', and
'Cathedral White' salvia**
(*Salvia farinacea* Cathedral
series), annual, perennial in
zones 7–10

**2 'Sweet Caroline Sweet-
heart Lime Green' sweet
potato** (*Ipomoea batatas*
'Sweet Caroline Sweetheart
Lime Green'), annual

Location: full sun, fertile
well-drained soil

Growing tip: Cut back the
sweet potatoes as needed
to keep in allotted space.

Season of performance:
summer through autumn

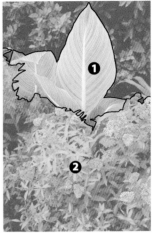

1 'Bengal Tiger' canna
(*Canna xgeneralis* 'Bengal Tiger'), zones 7–10

**2 'Anthony Waterer'
spiraea** (*Spiraea xbumalda* 'Anthony Waterer'), zones 3–8

Location: full sun or morning sun and midafternoon shade, fertile well-drained soil

Growing tip: 'Bengal Tiger' has orange flowers that usually don't show up until 'Anthony Waterer' is finished blooming. Of course, you can always grow a canna this colorful just for its foliage.

Season of performance: summer

Tiger Rose

'Bengal Tiger' canna has a lot of uses in the landscape, mostly for a tropical style, but this partnership is among the most unique and alluring. The variegated green leaves of 'Bengal Tiger' get more chartreuse in the morning sun and afternoon shade. The bold and flashy coarse-textured leaf makes the pink flowers of the 'Anthony Waterer' spiraea stand out more vibrantly, and instead of pastel they become hot rose pink.

A Torch for the Knight

1 'Purple Knight' alternanthera (*Alternanthera dentata* 'Purple Knight'), annual

2 'Torch Red Ember' gaillardia (*Gaillardia pulchella* 'Torch Red Ember'), annual

Location: full sun, fertile well-drained soil

Growing tip: 'Purple Knight' can reach 4 feet tall by autumn, but it responds well to any pruning you feel is necessary.

Season of performance: summer through autumn

The award-winning 'Purple Knight' is like a Joseph's coat on steroids. It is vigorous, never flinches in extreme heat and humidity, and can be the perfect complement to annuals, perennials, and tropicals. Here the fiery orange-red and yellow flowers of the 'Torch Red Ember' are even more colorful against the deep purple foliage of 'Purple Knight'. Gaillardias are strong performers, and they are loved by butterflies. 'Torch Red Ember' is a day-neutral plant, allowing it to bloom under the short days of autumn.

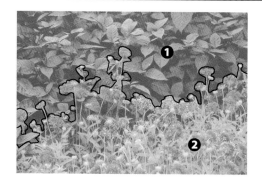

Trumpets and Daggers

Angel's trumpets have the ability to mesmerize all who gaze at their enormous flowers, which reach up to 18 inches in length. It's hard to believe these plants are related to tomatoes and peppers. In this rare partnership, they tower over the dagger-shaped 'Gold Garland' yucca. The green and creamy yellow variegated foliage gives the appearance of holding the trumpets at bay. Both the greens and yellows match in a harmonious marriage, yet this combination thrills with the incredible difference of textures.

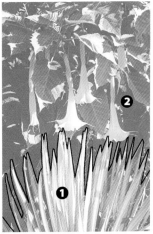

1 'Gold Garland' yucca (*Yucca filamentosa* 'Gold Garland'), zones 4–9

2 'Charles Grimaldi' angel's trumpet (*Brugmansia* 'Charles Grimaldi'), annual, perennial in zones (7) 8–10

Location: full to part sun, fertile well-drained soil

Growing tip: Angel's trumpets root easily, and it's not hard to maintain small plants over the winter.

Season of performance: summer and autumn

White Zinfandel with a Twist

1 'Sweet Caroline Light Green' sweet potato
(*Ipomoea batatas* 'Sweet Caroline Light Green'), annual

2 'Blanket Zinfandel' and 'Blanket White' petunia
(*Petunia* 'Blanket Zinfandel' and 'Blanket White'), annual

Location: full sun, moist fertile well-drained soil

Growing tip: If you have a wall, let the sweet potato drape over the edge. Use in baskets and containers as well.

Season of performance: late spring through early autumn

The deeply lobed lime green leaves of the 'Sweet Caroline Light Green' sweet potato make it one of the more striking foliage plants for the summer garden. It may be rugged and spreading, but it's also flashy. The small but very floriferous 'Blanket Zinfandel' and 'Blanket White' petunias are certainly capable of holding their own when it comes to attractiveness.

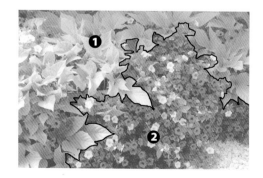

Foliage

In some combinations, we can leave out the flowering plants. Fabulous combinations can be grown with foliage only—the leaves and their partnership do it all. In many of these combinations, there's one dominant plant and the others either echo its color or provide such a stark contrast that the dominant plant appears even more beautiful.

If you were to drive through a tropical rain forest, you would notice huge plants and what seems an almost never-ending variety of leaf textures. By choosing plants for foliage we can create miniature versions of this look, changing the mundane city garden into a Garden of Eden.

Variegation also plays a prominent role in leaf texture. Gardeners can get overwhelmed with all of the new variegated forms released each year. Some forms may be considered gaudy or unattractive, but a good variegated plant adds great beauty and interest to the landscape. Plants like the lime green 'Blazin Lime' iresine can light up a shade garden, while the iridescent purple and silver Persian shield will cause visitors to pause and linger over its mesmerizing beauty.

When using foliage in the garden, your first inclination may be to simply spot plant. While this can be effective, the most pleasing results will most likely occur by planting in a similar fashion to the way you would perennials or annuals—plant in bold informal drifts of single colors or leaf textures. In other words, use a drift of hostas next to one of ferns or coleus.

Foliage plants also allow you to design in color schemes from monochromatic to complementary to triadic. No matter what your style or whether you have sun or shade, there are foliage plants that will allow you to have a garden that is sizzling.

The Blonde and the Doctor

1 'Stained Glassworks Big Blonde' coleus (*Solenostemon scutellarioides* 'Stained Glassworks Big Blonde'), annual

2 'Stained Glassworks Witch Doctor' coleus (*Solenostemon scutellarioides* 'Stained Glassworks Witch Doctor'), annual

Location: full sun to filtered light, fertile well-drained soil rich with organic matter

Growing tip: Keep leaves coming by feeding monthly with light applications of fertilizer.

Season of performance: summer through autumn

With coleuses like 'Stained Glassworks Big Blonde' and 'Stained Glassworks Witch Doctor' and a little planning, you can have a garden that has vibrant color all season. The chartreuse leaves of 'Big Blonde' tower above the exotic looking 'Witch Doctor', with leaves of the same color but with burgundy margins. The leaves of 'Witch Doctor' are so deeply serrated or lobed that they almost look like little fingers protruding outward. 'Witch Doctor' will be a talking point in your garden.

Burma Beauty

The Persian shield, native to Burma, is one of the most beautiful and unusual plants for tropical style gardens. Popular since Victorian times, it offers 8-inch-long leaves in iridescent shades of purple, lilac, and pink, with purplish maroon on the undersides. If those colors aren't awesome enough, the foliage looks like it has a light coat of electroplated silver. The colors seem to intensify when grown on the east side of giant plantain bananas, because the large leaves protect the Persian shield from scorching afternoon sun. The purple foliage contrasts strikingly with the large yellow trunks of the bananas.

1 Persian shield (*Strobilanthes dyerianus*), zones 8–11

2 Plantain banana (*Musa xparadisiaca*), zones (7) 8–11

Location: Morning sun and afternoon shade, well-drained soil rich with organic matter

Growing tip: After freezing, cut back and apply added mulch. The Japanese fiber banana (*Musa basjoo*) is a more cold hardy banana that would work as well.

Season of performance: summer and autumn

Cherry Lime

Lime or chartreuse plants continue to rock the garden world. Partner th[is] color with 'Aurora Black Cherry' and you have a spot in the filtered-light [or] part-shade garden that makes you want to pause and relax. 'Blazin Lim[e]' iresine is the perfect place to start. Native to tropical areas of South Amer[ica], it is related to Joseph's coat and reminiscent of the chicken gizzard or beefsteak plant our grandparents grew. The Aurora series of coleus i[s] compact and controlled, reaching only 12 inches tall.

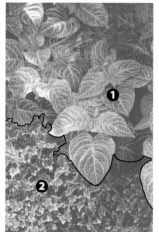

1 'Blazin Lime' iresine (*Iresine herbstii* 'Blazin Lime'), annual

2 'Aurora Black Cherry' coleus (*Solenostemon scutellarioides* 'Aurora Black Cherry'), annual

Location: filtered light or morning sun, fertile well-drained soil rich with organic matter

Growing tip: Feed monthly with light applications of a balanced fertilizer.

Season of performance: late spring through autumn

Chocolate Mint

'Chocolate Mint' coleus will indeed remind you of the fine chocolate you find on your hotel pillow. The large leaves are dark mahogany with lime green margins. Though many coleuses can take the sun, this is one for the shade. Here its partner is the flashy 'Limón' talinum or jewels of Opar, which is capable of growing in sun or shade. Its leaves are dark lime in shade and light lime in sun. 'Limón' also produces hot pink flowers that resemble baby's breath and are perfect for cutting.

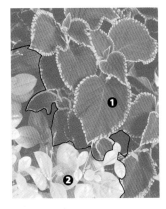

1 'Chocolate Mint' coleus (*Solenostemon scutellarioides* 'Chocolate Mint'), annual

2 'Limón' talinum (*Talinum paniculatum* 'Limón'), annual, perennial (8) 9–11

Location: shade or filtered light, fertile well-drained soil

Growing tip: Use 'Chocolate Mint' with 'Sum and Substance' hosta and 'Lime Zinger' elephant ear.

Season of performance: summer through autumn

Electric Pearls

The dark purple leaves of the All-America Selections winner 'Black Pearl' ornamental pepper go with just about any color, and in this combination the pepper ties the planting together. The 'Electric Lime' coleus, which practically seems to be glowing, is almost a direct complement to the pepper, yet the shiny silvery leaves of the dichondra are also right at home in the combination. Here 'Silver Falls' shows its ability to function well as a groundcover, but it also excels in baskets, where it gives a vertical element falling downward as much as your comfort zone will allow.

1 'Electric Lime' coleus
(*Solenostemon scutellarioides* 'Electric Lime'), annual

2 'Black Pearl' pepper
(*Capsicum annuum* 'Black Pearl'), annual

3 'Silver Falls' dichondra
(*Dichondra argentea* 'Silver Falls'), annual

Location: full sun, moist fertile well-drained soil

Growing tip: Keep 'Electric Lime' pinched back and the plant will have a terrific bushy habit.

Season of performance: summer through autumn

Fantasy with Foli

This dazzling bed is packed with color, all of it from foliage. 'Blazin Rose' iresine or beefsteak plant and 'Sweet Caroline Light Green' sweet potato are the two standout performers here, but as the coleus continue to reach their potential, the bed will be as colorful as a Caribbean carnival. The long and thin 'Pink Chaos' ties into both the iresine and sweet potato with its lime green margins and hot pink centers. The brightly variegated leaves of 'Merlin's Magic' also echo the colors.

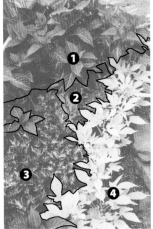

1 'Blazin Rose' iresine (*Iresine herbstii* 'Blazin Rose'), annual

2 'Pink Chaos' coleus (*Solenostemon scutellarioides* 'Pink Chaos'), annual

3 'Merlin's Magic' coleus (*Solenostemon scutellarioides* 'Merlin's Magic'), annual

4 'Sweet Caroline Light Green' sweet potato (*Ipomoea batatas* 'Sweet Caroline Light Green'), annual

Location: morning and filtered afternoon sun, fertile soil rich with organic matter

Growing tip: Cut back sweet potato as needed for direction of growth and to keep in allotted space.

Season of performance: summer through autumn

Flaming Foliage

When the 'Tropicanna' canna made its debut with its flaming foliage, [it] gave notice to the world that the canna was back. With leaves that riva[l] a croton in color, who cares if it ever blooms? The stripes of red, orange[,] yellow, and green give the garden a coarse texture that's unsurpassed. The 'Rustic Orange' coleus lends a simpler but no less colorful leaf of orang[e] with margins of gold. The lighter but similar color of the coleus furthe[r] strengthens the appeal of the flamboyant 'Tropicanna'.

1 'Rustic Orange' coleus (*Solenostemon scutellarioides* 'Rustic Orange'), annual

2 'Tropicanna' canna (*Canna xgeneralis* 'Tropicanna'), zones 7–10

Location: full to part sun, fertile well-drained soil rich with organic matter

Growing tip: In areas colder than zone 7, 'Tropicanna' can be easily dug and stored for the winter.

Season of performance: summer through autumn

Judy, Judy, Judy

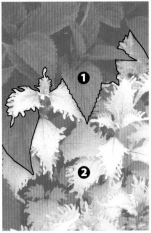

ary Grant was credited with saying "Judy, Judy, Judy," but never really said
. Had he grown 'Big Red Judy' coleus in his garden, there's no telling what
e might have said. This selection gets large, reaching 3 feet, with leaves
 deep, rich, vibrant red. The awesome partner in this bed is 'Lemon Sun-
ation' coleus, whose yellow leaves with hints of chartreuse alone makes
: a good contrasting combination. But the stems, margins, and veins of
Lemon Sunsation' are the same color as the leaves of 'Big Red Judy', tying
he combination together.

1 'Big Red Judy' coleus
(*Solenostemon scutellarioides* 'Big Red Judy'), annual

**2 'Lemon Sunsation'
coleus** (*Solenostemon
scutellarioides* 'Lemon Sunsation'), annual

Location: full sun or filtered light, fertile moist soil
rich with organic matter

Growing tip: Keep these
coleus watered as needed.
Feed them a little, and
remove any flowers that
start to form.

Season of performance:
summer through autumn

New Guinea Magic

Nestled among the giant plantain bananas, the 'Tricolor' caricature plant becomes a most picturesque partner in the tropical landscape. The green leaves of 'Tricolor' are among the more exotic in the garden world, featuring variegation that's made of an irregular band of cream with a touch of orange in the middle of the leaf. The deep shrimp pink stems also make an impact. If the caricature plant gets backlit by the sun, they almost look like they are glowing.

1 'Tricolor' caricature plant (*Graptophyllum pictum* 'Tricolor'), annual, perennial in zones 10–11

2 Plantain banana (*Musa xparadisiaca*), zones (7) 8–11

Location: full to part sun, fertile moist soil rich with organic matter

Growing tip: The caricature plant can grow in sun or shade.

Season of performance: summer through autumn

Stained Glass

It's hard to believe you can have a garden this colorful and easy to grow just by planting coleus. Green and red are natural opposites, but this fiery contrast between 'Big Blonde' and 'Molten Lava' is extraordinarily flashy. The smaller but spreading 'Burgundy Wedding Train' has been one of the top performers in trials across the country. Its margins match the color of 'Big Blonde'.

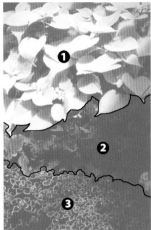

1 'Stained Glassworks Big Blonde' coleus (*Solenostemon scutellarioides* 'Stained Glassworks Big Blonde'), annual

2 'Stained Glassworks Molten Lava' coleus (*Solenostemon scutellarioides* 'Stained Glassworks Molten Lava'), annual

3 'Stained Glassworks Burgundy Wedding Train' coleus (*Solenostemon scutellarioides* 'Stained Glassworks Burgundy Wedding Train'), annual

Location: full to part sun, fertile well-drained soil

Growing tip: Keep flower buds pinched to stimulate growth and keep bushy.

Season of performance: summer through autumn

Storm over Miami

There are only a handful of plants with foliage such a blazing colorful red as the Great American Cities 'Miami Storm'. Any flowers are inconsequential on such a beautiful plant. The deeply saturated red is the perfect complement for the dark green of the cut-leaf philodendron. 'Miami Storm' reaches about 12 inches tall, and plants need to be spaced 10 inches apart. Tucking them in with philodendrons creates a tropical look, but also try combining these begonias with hostas, toad lily, and Solomon's seal.

1 Cut-leaf philodendron
(*Philodendron bipinnatifidum*), zones (8) 9–11

2 'Miami Storm' begonia (*Begonia rex-cultorum* 'Miami Storm'), annual

Location: morning sun and afternoon shade or filtered light, moist fertile soil rich with organic matter

Growing tip: 'Miami Storm' can be grown indoors during the winter; give it high humidity and bright indirect light. This begonia does not go dormant, so don't let it dry out.

Season of performance: late spring through autumn

Tranquil Retreat

This courtyard garden is soothing and inviting with its color scheme of mauves and greens. It also has an interesting variety of textures, from the fine-leafed grass to the statuesque structure of the Japanese loquat with its leathery semi-glossy leaves. The 'Saturn' coleus echoes the lime green of the 'Marguerite' sweet potato and the mauve of the grass.

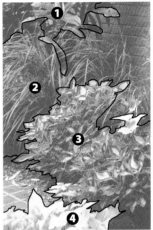

1 Japanese loquat (*Erio-botrya japonica***)**, zones (7) 8–10

2 Purple fountain grass (*Pennisetum setaceum*), annual, perennial in zones 9–11

3 'Saturn' coleus (*Sole-nostemon scutellarioides* 'Saturn'), annual

4 'Marguerite' sweet potato (*Ipomoea batatas* 'Marguerite'), annual

Location: full to part sun, fertile well-drained soil rich with organic matter

Growing tip: The loquat blooms in late autumn with delicious fruit ripening in spring, provided they don't all freeze during the winter.

Season of performance: summer through autumn

Herbs

In general, an herb is a plant with nonwoody stems, though we usually think of herbs as having culinary uses. When you mention herbs for the landscape, your first thought may be tomatoes in the flowerbed in the summer. But whether its summer or winter, new selections of vegetables and herbs are making the flower border more aesthetically enjoyable and in many cases tasty, too. Some butterflies and hummingbirds are attracted to herbs, and dill and fennel are favorite foods for some caterpillars. This chapter covers all sorts of leafy vegetables and herbs, including some for which the entire plant—roots and all—are edible. Others, like flowering kale, produce leaves that are attractive and can be used as garnishes. Herbs have become popular and are real landscape assets, even if they do have culinary properties.

Most of these plants thrive in well-drained soil that has a pH of 6.0 to 6.8 for optimum growth. Proper drainage can be achieved by working in organic matter or filling raised beds with a prepared soil mix. A proper nutritional balance is important for good growth. Too much fertilizer causes succulent growth, leading to less flavor as well as plants that tend to lose some weather toughness, disease resistance, and drought tolerance. It's a good idea to feed with regular light applications of fertilizer during the growing season. The winter-growing crops will make better use of dilute water-soluble fertilizer than granules, whose release is tied to soil temperature and rain. Be aware that some herbs grow tall and need to be placed toward the back of the border.

Though we don't eat many of the sage or salvia selections, most are highly aromatic when harvested. These can be tied in bundles with a few sprigs of rosemary, a decorative ribbon, and hung in the kitchen. Pansies and violas are edible, and they combine wonderfully with plants like mus-

tard and cardoon as well as with snapdragon relatives. Each spring and autumn garden centers offer a broad selection of herbs and edibles for immediate planting in the garden or landscape. There is no rule that says you can't give them a prominent place.

Bees, Butterflies, and Bouquets

Anise hyssop is a special herb that yields edible flowers, flavoring for teas, and seeds for cookies and attracts butterflies and bees by the scores. The vibrant blue flowers are also prized in the landscape. Here they harmonize in a delightful trio with 'Bouquet Purple' dianthus, an award-winning cut flower, and 'Cooler Mix' periwinkles known for summer perseverance.

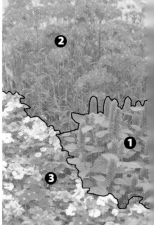

1 'Honey Bee Blue' anise hyssop (*Agastache foeniculum* 'Honey Bee Blue'), annual, perennial in zones 5–9

2 'Bouquet Purple' dianthus (*Dianthus barbatus* interspecific hybrid 'Bouquet Purple'), zones 4–9

3 'Cooler Mix' periwinkle (*Catharanthus roseus* 'Cooler Mix'), annual

Location: full to part sun, fertile well-drained soil

Growing tip: 'Honey Bee Blue' responds well to cutting back, so feel free to do so if the plants begin to look a little leggy or you want them to be bushier.

Season of performance: summer through early autumn

Cuisine for a Princess

The princess flower, which has been blooming all summer, towers over this cool-season landscape like royalty gathering her subjects. The 'Amazon Rose Magic' dianthus, bearing tall stems of white, pink, and rose, is rare in that some of its flowers contrast while others harmonize with the purple. The edible Swiss chard acts as a colorful leafy groundcover that yields leaves that can be eaten like spinach—fresh in salad or cooked—and stems that are treated like asparagus.

1 Princess flower (*Tibouchina urvilleana*), annual, perennial in zones 8–11

2 'Amazon Rose Magic' dianthus (*Dianthus barbatus* interspecific hybrid 'Amazon Rose Magic'), annual, perennial in zones 6–8b

3 'Bright Lights' Swiss chard (*Beta vulgaris* 'Bright Lights'), annual

Location: full to part sun, fertile well-drained soil rich with organic matter

Growing tip: Plant 'Bright Lights' 6 inches apart and feed regularly during the growing season.

Season of performance: autumn

The Eyes Have It

This garden is a lesson in varying texture with harmony in leaf color, but it's those eyes that catch your glance. The golden and red blossoms of the 'Peek-a-Boo' eyeball or toothache plant complement the Russian sage, with its violet blue spires and olive grayish green leaves as well with the silver gray of the 'Powis Castle' artemisia and fuzzy lambs ear.

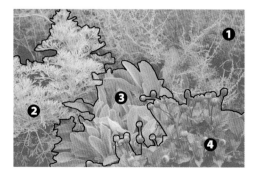

1 Russian sage (*Perovskia atriplicifolia*), zones 4–9

2 'Powis Castle' artemisia (*Artemisia* 'Powis Castle'), zones 5–8

3 Lambs ear (*Stachys byzantina*), zones 4–8

4 'Peek-a-Boo' eyeball plant (*Acmella oleracea* 'Peek-a-Boo'), annual, perennial in zones 10–11

Location: full to part sun, very well-drained soil

Growing tip: All of these plants are drought tolerant once established, so don't overwater.

Season of performance: summer through autumn

Fans and Flavor

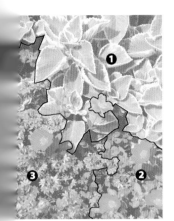

Cuban oregano is fueling a new and increasingly popular trend of growing herbs in the landscape. Here it provides a saucy contrast to the scores of intensely blue violet fan flowers of the scaevola, and it sets the stage for the purslane to boldly grab attention with its fiery scarlet blooms. You'll grow Cuban oregano for its fuzzy texture and amazing fragrance, and soon you'll be researching recipes for culinary use.

1 Cuban oregano
(*Plectranthus amboinicus*), annual, perennial in zones 10–11

2 'Rio Scarlet' purslane
(*Portulaca oleracea* 'Rio Scarlet'), annual

3 'Whirlwind Blue' fan flower (*Scaevola aemula* 'Whirlwind Blue'), annual, perennial in zones 9–11

Location: full to part sun, fertile moist well-drained soil

Growing tip: Pinch or cut back Cuban oregano as needed to maintain shape and size.

Season of performance: summer and autumn

Fine and Furry

Fine texture and big furry leaves offer everything you could want in two foliage plants. The silver sage, a short-lived perennial (sometimes referred to as a biennial), produces large silvery leaves. The silver comes from the fine hairs and stands out in stark contrast to the bronze fennel, with its extra-fine leaf texture. Bronze fennel is a culinary delight, with aromatic leaves and seeds that are used in Italian dishes, and it's also great in the butterfly garden. The umbels of tiny yellow flowers are showy.

1 Silver sage (*Salvia argentea*), annual, perennial in zones 5–8

2 Brown fennel (*Foeniculum vulgare*), annual, perennial in zones 5–11

Location: full to part sun, well-drained soil

Growing tip: To keep bronze fennel bushy, cut foliage back as needed until you are ready for it to produce flowers and seed.

Season of performance: spring through autumn

Garnish to Gourmet

This garden provides everything: bouquets for the vase from the 'Amazon Rose Magic' dianthus, garnishes for the table from the colorful flowering kale, and tasty gourmet dishes from the cardoon, a globe artichoke relative. It goes without saying you'll have a dramatic cool-season landscape, too. The pinks and purples work in harmony, while the whites and grays contrast beautifully.

1 Cardoon (*Cynara cardunculus*), annual, perennial in zones 6–11

2 'Amazon Rose Magic' dianthus (*Dianthus barbatus* interspecific hybrid 'Amazon Rose Magic'), annual, perennial in zones 6–8b

3 'Chidori Red' and 'Chidori White' flowering kale (*Brassica oleracea* 'Chidori Red' and 'Chidori White'), annuals

Location: full to part sun, fertile well-drained soil

Growing tip: Flowering kale is very cold hardy. Once acclimated, it can take bone-chilling temperatures below zero. Completely cover with pine straw if needed during those especially cold periods.

Season of performance: autumn through spring

I'm OK, You're OK

This garden would be the proverbial poster representing "have fun gardening." Plant what you like. It's fine to put a tomato in your flower border or plant nasturtiums to eat in your salads or to pickle. Nasturtium leaves are eaten in salads like watercress. This garden of different shades of greens and opposite reds holds your interest, and the vertical elements of the 'Red Sensation' cordyline create excitement.

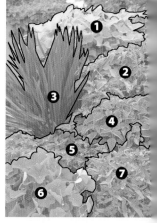

1 'Marguerite' ornamental sweet potato (*Ipomoea batatas* 'Marguerite'), annual

2 Tomato (*Solanum lycopersicum* cv.), annual

3 'Red Sensation' cordyline (*Cordyline australis* 'Red Sensation'), annual, perennial in zones 7–9

4 'Rustic Orange' coleus (*Solenostemon scutellarioides* 'Rustic Orange'), annual

5 'Lucky Red Hot Improved' lantana (*Lantana camara* 'Lucky Red Hot Improved'), annual, perennial in zones 8–10

6 'Whirlybird' nasturtium (*Tropaeolum majus* 'Whirlybird'), annual

7 'Profusion Knee High Red' zinnia (*Zinnia* 'Profusion Knee High Red'), annual

Location: full sun, fertile well-drained soil

Growing tip: Vigorous plants may need to be pinched or cut to keep in their allotted space.

Season of performance: spring, summer and autumn

Incredible Edible

'Red Giant' mustard has come out of nowhere to become one of the hottest plants for the edible landscape or to be a simply dazzling foliage plant for autumn and winter. Mustards can be planted in the autumn or early spring, while the primula is usually an early spring planting. They're strikingly beautiful in the landscape partnered with primulas, such as the Prima series pictured. The burgundy red starts to develop as temperatures get below 60F, intensifying as it gets colder and making the landscape pop. The 'Red Giant' mustard is tasty when cooked like other mustard greens.

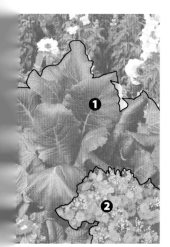

1 'Red Giant' mustard
(*Brassica juncea* var. *rugosa* 'Red Giant'), annual

2 'Prima Rose with Eye' primula (*Primula malacoides* 'Prima Rose with Eye'), annual

Location: full to part sun, fertile well-drained soil rich with organic matter

Growing tip: Keep the 'Red Giant' mustard growing vigorously with supplemental water during cold dry periods and light applications of water-soluble fertilizer every 4 to 6 weeks.

Season of performance: spring through early summer

Lights in the Landscape

'Bright Lights' are coming on in landscapes everywhere, from homes to office buildings and malls. Eat the leaves like spinach and cook the stems like asparagus. The plants have attractive stems and leaves in yellow, orange, pinkish violet, burgundy, and red. Here it is combined with a giant taro elephant ear in a tropical style setting. Backlit by the sun, the chard leaves reveal a kaleidoscope of colors.

1 'Bright Lights' Swiss chard (*Beta vulgaris* 'Bright Lights'), annual

2 Giant taro elephant ear (*Alocasia macrorrhiza*), annual, perennial in zones 8–11

Location: full to part sun, fertile well-drained soil

Growing tip: Plant 'Bright Lights' in drifts 6 inches apart and feed with a dilute water-soluble fertilizer every couple of weeks during the growing season. Elephant ears are easily dug and stored if needed.

Season of performance: autumn through spring

Lucky Girl

This young girl is standing pretty in a field of pure silver. She is surrounded by fragrant artemisias, one of the most loved herbs in the world. The famous French tarragon is also an artemisia, and these herbs are used medicinally as well as to flavor liqueurs and culinary dishes. This fragrant garden of silver is topped off with the silver-leafed iridescent red flowers of the rose campion, whose blooms last until early summer.

1 Rose campion (Lychnis coronaria), zones 3–8

2 'Powis Castle' artemisia (Artemisia 'Powis Castle'), zones 5–8

3 Western mugwort artemisia (*Artemisia ludoviciana*), zones 4–9

Location: full to part sun, luxuriant soil not necessary but good drainage is essential

Growing tip: Once artemisias get woody, cut back to rejuvenate lush growth.

Season of performance: late spring through summer

Mona and Magilla

Perillas and plectranthus have been in herb gardens for decades, and now they are in the flower garden, too. 'Magilla Vanilla' is large and bushy with green and cream variegation that complements any partner. But you could hardly improve on 'Mona Lavender'. This member of the mint family amazes with beautiful spikes of lavender flowers all summer. The leaves are uniquely dark green with purple undersides. The 'Cabaret Yellow' calibrachoa is also an artistic complement for the lavender blooms.

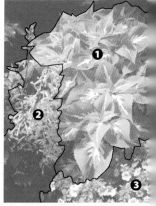

1 'Magilla Vanilla' perilla (*Perilla* 'Magilla Vanilla'), annual, perennial in zones 10–11

2 'Mona Lavender' plectranthus (*Plectranthus* 'Mona Lavender'), annual, perennial in zones 10–11

3 'Cabaret Yellow' calibrachoa (*Calibrachoa* 'Cabaret Yellow'), annual, perennial in zones (7) 8–11

Location: morning sun and afternoon shade, fertile soil rich with organic matter

Growing tip: Remove spent flowers from 'Mona Lavender' and cut back perilla as needed.

Season of performance: summer through autumn

Moroccan Marvel

Cardoon, a perennial native to Morocco, is sweeping the country in popularity. This globe artichoke relative with deeply toothed soft gray-green foliage is engaging in the cool-season landscape until late spring and early summer. Young tender stems may be eaten like celery, the leaves like spinach, and the main root sautéed in butter. In midsummer, cardoon produces 6-foot-tall spikes with thistle-like, blue-violet blooms. After blooming the plant dies, returning in the autumn. In this portrait-like setting cardoon is used similarly to flowering kale and is partnered with 'Matrix Ocean Breeze Mix' pansies and 'Amazon Rose Magic' dianthus.

1 Cardoon (*Cynara cardunculus*), annual, perennial in zones 6–11

2 'Matrix Ocean Breeze Mix' pansy (*Viola* x*wittrockiana* 'Matrix Ocean Breeze Mix'), annual

3 'Amazon Rose Magic' dianthus (*Dianthus barbatus* interspecific hybrid 'Amazon Rose Magic'), annual, perennial in zones 6–8b

Location: full to part sun, deep fertile soil

Growing tip: Cardoon can easily form a 3-foot-wide clump, so give it room.

Season of performance: autumn through spring

Peek-a-Boo, I See You

'Peek-a-Boo' will get children interested in gardening, as the plant looks like an alien in the garden looking at them or a plant with eyeballs. Often called eyeball plant, the 'Peek-a-Boo' flower is a golden, olive-sized ball with a round red eye. The dark green and bronze foliage is edible, with a peppery taste when used in salads. It's also called toothache plant because the leaves and flowers have a numbing effect when chewed. Here it's combined with the silvery fine-leafed 'Powis Castle' artemisia for a textural extravaganza.

1 'Peek-a-Boo' eyeball plant (*Acmella oleracea* 'Peek-a-Boo'), annual, perennial in zones 10–11

2 'Powis Castle' artemisia (*Artemisia* 'Powis Castle'), zones 5–8

Location: full to part sun, well-drained soil

Growing tip: 'Peek-a-Boo' likes frequent light applications of fertilizer.

Season of performance: summer through autumn

A Planting to Purr About

Looking like a rolling sea in the wind, 'Walker's Low' catmint's crinkly aromatic foliage with blue violet flowers is a delight in the herb or perennial garden. Don't let this selection's name fool you, however, it reaches 36 inches tall with an equal spread. Once established, it is drought-tolerant, resistant to deer and rabbits, and has few pests or diseases. Partner it with the complementing 'Moonshine' yarrow and you'll have a garden that's beautiful, tough, and suitable for harvesting or drying.

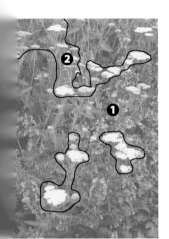

1 'Walker's Low' catmint
(*Nepeta xfaassenii* 'Walker's Low'), zones 3–8

2 'Moonshine' yarrow
(*Achillea* 'Moonshine'), zones 3–9

Location: full sun but some afternoon shade in hot climates is appreciated, well-drained soil

Growing tip: It blooms almost continuously from May until frost if pruned back by two-thirds when initial flowers fade.

Season of performance: summer through autumn

Photo courtesy of the Perennial Plant Association

Salmon and Mustard

'Red Giant' mustard's deep burgundy leaves bring beauty to the edible landscape. While almost any color will work as a partner, the warm hues of the 'Ultima Salmon Yellow' pansy provide a companionship of rare cool-season beauty. The red tones make the deep apricot color blend perfectly with the mustard leaves. 'Ultima Salmon Yellow' pansies are about 2 inches across but pack a lot of flower power. As with all mustards, the young tender leaves make the best greens.

1 'Red Giant' mustard (*Brassica juncea* var. *rugosa* 'Red Giant'), annual

2 'Ultima Salmon Yellow' pansy (*Viola xwittrockiana* 'Ultima Salmon Yellow'), annual

Location: full to part sun, fertile well-drained soil rich with organic matter

Growing tip: If you are plagued with tight heavy soil, working in peat will give you much better success with cool-season crops.

Season of performance: autumn through spring

Taste of Tropical Oregano

Cuban oregano, Spanish thyme, and Mexican mint are all names for a tough-as-nails plant for the landscape, container, or herb garden. Here the green leaves with contrasting white margins intermingle with the 'Profusion Fire' zinnia. The Profusion series has put the fun back into growing zinnias, with their award-winning performance and disease resistance. This garden combination is easy to grow, providing aroma for passersby and a great herb for the culinary artist of the home.

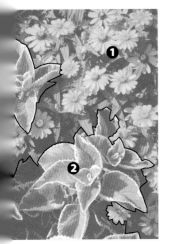

1 'Profusion Fire' zinnia
(*Zinnia* 'Profusion Fire'), annual

2 Cuban oregano
(*Plectranthus amboinicus*), annual, perennial in zones 10–11

Location: full sun, fertile moist well-drained soil

Growing tip: Use Cuban oregano near areas that you frequent, so you can enjoy its fragrance.

Season of performance: summer through autumn

Cottage

There is a revival of sorts going on in the world of gardening, and it's all around us. It's the revival of the cottage garden. In some places cottage gardens never left, but now this style of garden is popping up in rural areas as well as in new neighborhoods with the most modern homes.

Included in this revival of style comes the old-fashioned picket fence. The fence may be white or natural and it serves multiple purposes, as it did for our ancestors. Sure, it may keep in the pooch, but the picket fence is an architectural element that defines spaces and edges in the garden and acts as a support structure for vines like the coral honeysuckle, clematis, and even the mandevilla in the tropical cottage garden. In addition to vines, you'll find antique roses like 'New Dawn', 'Mermaid', and 'Madame Isaac Pereire' and newer English rose selections like 'Abraham Darby', 'Evelyn', and 'Graham Thomas' draping these fences with fragrance and elegance. The classic wooden bench is also showing up in cottage gardens, as gardeners realize it's a thing of beauty as well as the perfect spot for a cup of morning coffee and a brief rest.

No two cottage gardens are alike, because there are no rules to follow. The common thread seems to be a love for picket fences and flowers of all sorts, from those that are tall and spiky textured to round blooms. Plants grown for foliage also have become increasingly popular. Artwork seems to be the finishing touch of the cottage garden. As you'll see, the artwork can be handmade, recycled, or crafted by the finest artisans. Without yard art, statuary, or ironwork, something is missing. The artwork in a cottage garden is like the signature on a masterful painting. How will you sign yours?

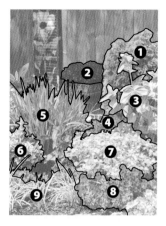

Artisan Cottage

The large drift of tough-as-nails melampodium bloom throughout the summer into autumn, complementing the adjacent coleus and Easy Wave petunias. The recycled shutter with a hand-painted flower enhances this outdoor room in a similar fashion to a fine painting hanging on the wall in the living room. Color and texture abound in this unique cottage garden. The combination of grasses, round flowers, spiky flowers, sword-like foliage, and evergreens creates a garden that is pleasing and visually stimulating.

1 Hinoki false cypress (*Chamaecyparis obtusa*), zones 5–8

2 'Purple Ruffles' basil (*Ocimum basilicum* 'Purple Ruffles'), annual

3 Zinnia (*Zinnia violacea* cv.), annual

4 Coleus (*Solenostemon scutellarioides* cv.), annual

5 Crocosmia (*Crocosmia* xcrocosmiiflora), zones 5–10

6 'Aureo-marginata' golden euonymus (*Euonymus japonica* 'Aureo-marginata'), zones 6–10

7 'Million Gold' melampodium (*Melampodium divaricatum* 'Million Gold'), annual

8 'Easy Wave Blue' and 'Easy Wave Pink' petunias (*Petunia* 'Easy Wave Blue' and 'Pink Wave Pink'), annual

9 'Silvery Sunproof' liriope (*Liriope muscari* 'Silvery Sunproof'), zones 6–10

Location: full to part sun, fertile well-drained soil

Growing tip: Train your plants to establish deep roots by watering deeply but less often

Season of performance: summer through autumn

Autumn in the Delta

This garden offers a variety of plant textures, from the grassy plumes of the pampas grass to spiky and round flowers, but sometimes the artwork just makes a cottage garden. This garden, which no doubt has an abundance of butterflies and hummingbirds, also has two life-sized copper kids trying to catch bees around the giant sunflowers. This artwork combined with the showy salvias and autumn-blooming mums creates a festive atmosphere in this Mississippi delta garden.

1 Mexican bush sage (*Salvia leucantha*), annual, perennial in zones 7b–10

2 Chrysanthemum (Chrysanthemum cv.), zones 5–9

3 Papaya (Carica papaya), annual, perennial in zones 10–11

4 Pampas grass (*Cortaderia selloana*), zones 5–10

5 'Lady in Red' salvia (*Salvia coccinea* 'Lady in Red'), reseeding annual, perennial in zones 9–10

6 'Indigo Spires' salvia (*Salvia* 'Indigo Spires'), zones 7–11

Location: full sun, fertile well-drained soil

Growing tip: The perennials are grown on raised beds for good winter drainage.

Season of performance: summer and autumn

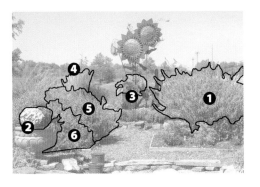

California Style Spring Cottage

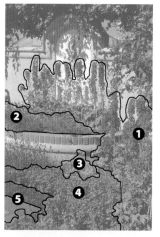

As their name suggests, the 'Guardian Blue' delphiniums stand like sentries watching over the rest of the spring garden. Blue is such a sought-after color in the garden, and when it's atop plants reaching over 3 feet tall you have a wow effect in the garden. The blue complements the fiery orange of the fragrant 'Citrona Orange'. But fragrance is everywhere in this cottage garden as the linaria, nemesia, and alyssum all entice you to linger.

1 'Guardian Blue' delphinium (*Delphinium elatum* 'Guardian Blue'), zones 4–8

2 'Enchantment' linaria (*Linaria* 'Enchantment'), annual

3 'Citrona Orange' erysimum (*Erysimum* 'Citrona Orange'), annual

4 'Poetry Blue' nemesia (*Nemesia foetens* 'Poetry Blue'), annual

5 'Easter Bonnet Violet' alyssum (*Lobularia maritima* 'Easter Bonnet Violet'), annual

Location: full to part sun, fertile well-drained soil

Growing tip: Stake the delphiniums while young, and cut old flower stalks to encourage repeat blooms.

Season of performance: spring and early summer

Camelot Cottage

Reaching 4 feet tall, the 'Camelot' foxglove is the quintessential cottage garden plant. The spikes of tubular flowers stand tall and picturesque. In addition to their beauty, foxgloves are also a leading source of food for darting and acrobatic hummingbirds. The perfect complement just might be the award-winning 'May Night' salvia, with spiky blue violet flowers that are loved by both hummingbirds and butterflies. Both also make great cut flowers.

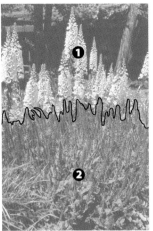

1 'Camelot Cream' foxglove (*Digitalis purpurea* 'Camelot Cream'), zones 4–8

2 'May Night' salvia (*Salvia* x*sylvestris* 'May Night'), zones 4–8

Location: sun to part sun, fertile well-drained soil

Growing tip: 'Camelot Cream' forms large clumps and prefers a little afternoon shade in hotter climates. Quickly cutting spent flowers on 'May Night' will encourage more blooms.

Season of performance: late spring and summer

Caribbean Cottage

Mention cottage style gardening and the first thought may be thatched roof homes in England or colonial Williamsburg, but they're also popular on islands like St. Barthélemy or Saba. Anyone can make a Caribbean style cottage garden by choosing the right plants. Here the coarse-textured foliage of the banana looks so lush and the tropical mandevilla on the glistening white fence sets the mood. Partnered with vinca, a summer staple, and you have the look of the islands.

1 Edible plantain banana (*Musa xparadisiaca*), zones (7) 8–10

2 'Alice du Pont' mandevilla (*Mandevilla xamabilis* 'Alice du Pont'), annual, perennial in zones 9–11

3 'Titan Mix' vinca (*Catharanthus roseus* 'Titan Mix'), annual

Location: full sun, fertile well-drained soil

Growing tip: Plant vincas after the soil has warmed in late spring. Feed the mandevilla monthly with light applications of fertilizer.

Season of performance: summer and early autumn

Classic Cottage

A picket fence, classic bench, spiky flowers, round flowers, feathery plumes, and a native blooming vine loved by hummingbirds makes this a cottage garden for the ages. The 8-inch tall woven grapevine edging separating the sidewalk and garden adds a unique natural charm to the garden. Although a stained bench has its place, the aged and weathered bench does too and beckons us to sit, relax, and enjoy the surroundings.

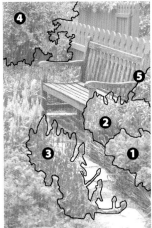

1 Marigold (*Tagetes patula* cv.), annual

2 'Victoria Blue' mealy-cup sage (*Salvia farinacea* 'Victoria Blue'), annual, perennial in zones 7–10

3 Celosia (*Celosia plumosa* cv.), annual

4 Coral honeysuckle (*Lonicera sempervirens*), zones 4–9

5 Brown-eyed Susan (*Rudbeckia triloba*), zones 5–9

Location: full sun, fertile well-drained soil

Growing tip: Late summer marigolds, zinnias, and dwarf sunflowers can bring fresh and vibrant color until frost arrives in the autumn.

Season of performance: summer through autumn

Cottage Nouveau

1 'Mermaid' rose (*Rosa* 'Mermaid'), zones 7–10

2 Larkspur (*Consolida ajacis*), reseeding annual

3 Ox-eye daisy (*Leucanthemum vulgare*), zones 3–8

4 'Coronation Gold' yarrow (*Achillea* 'Coronation Gold'), zones 3–9

5 'Pinkie' rose (*Rosa* 'Pinkie'), zones 6–9

6 'Early Sunrise' coreopsis (*Coreopsis grandiflora* 'Early Sunrise'), zones 4–9

Location: full sun, well-drained soil

Growing tip: 'Mermaid' is a rose that can tolerate more shade than most and still perform beautifully.

Season of performance: late spring and summer

This glistening white picket fence is adorned with the 'Mermaid' rose, which made its debut in 1918. People long remember the saucer-sized fragrant blooms of this selection. Picket fences are idyllic backdrops for flowers such as these tall blue larkspurs, which complement both the coreopsis and the gold yarrow. As visitors walk around the large garden, they are greeted by drifts of 'Pinkie' roses and ox-eye daisies ready for cutting.

Daisy Days in the Garden

Shimmering white daisies and orange coreopsis make a marriage that young and old find irresistible. The daisies also have orange centers, enhancing the partnership. You could hardly find a better pair for the spring and early summer cottage garden, as both attract butterflies and make good cut flowers. This combination also works in the traditional perennial garden or naturalized wildflower meadow, too.

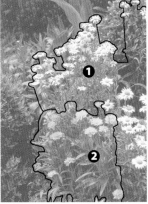

1 Ox-eye daisy (*Leucanthemum vulgare*), zones 3–8

2 'Early Sunrise' coreopsis (*Coreopsis grandiflora* 'Early Sunrise'), zones 4–9

Location: full to part sun, well-drained soil, luxuriant soil is not necessary

Growing tip: The ox-eye daisy can spread by underground rhizomes, so pay attention to unwanted volunteers. Deadheading spent flowers of the coreopsis aids in disease prevention.

Season of performance: spring and summer

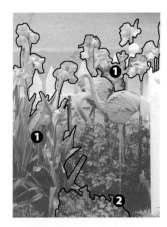

1 Bearded iris (*Iris* cv.), zones 3–10

2 'Telstar Coral' dianthus (*Dianthus barbatus* x *chinensis* 'Telstar Coral'), annual, perennial in zones 5–8

Location: full sun, fertile well-drained soil rich with organic matter

Growing tip: Dividing iris every 3 to 4 years is vital to flower production.

Season of performance: spring

Dance of the Flamingoes

Sometimes it's the yard art that makes the cottage garden—actually, any garden. It's kind of like the icing on the cake. The white picket fence is an integral part of the garden, for sure, but the appearance of the pink flamingoes feeding among the flowers creates the perfect look. The fragrant dianthus with its partnering coral pink color completes the garden. Notice, however, it's the old-fashioned bearded irises that tower above the flamingos and garner the attention.

Dawn of the Cottage Garden

This garden typifies the old-fashioned cottage in every aspect, from the rustic wood, pass-a-long purple-leafed perilla, to the deutzia starting to bloom on the right. The colorful mix of pansies may be showy, but it's the climbing 'New Dawn' rose that takes your breath away. This selection made its debut in 1930. Its magnificent blooms appear in the spring and repeat in the summer. It's also fragrant, another reason why 'New Dawn' is highly sought after today. Climbers on a wall, trellis, or arbor add unparalleled charm to a cottage garden.

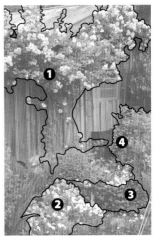

1 'New Dawn' rose (*Rosa* 'New Dawn'), zones 5–9

2 Pansy (*Viola* xwittrockiana cv.), annual

3 Purple perilla (*Perilla frutescens*), annual

4 Deutzia (*Deutzia* cv.), zones 4–9

Location: full to part sun, fertile well-drained soil rich with organic matter

Growing tip: Though called climbing roses, these selections do require your help by tying and training.

Season of performance: spring and summer

Hedgehogs and Mopheads

1 'Kim's Mophead' purple coneflower (*Echinacea purpurea* 'Kim's Mophead'), zones 3–8

2 'Kim's Knee High' purple coneflower (*Echinacea purpurea* 'Kim's Knee High'), zones 3–8

3 'Little Boy' phlox (*Phlox paniculata* 'Little Boy'), zones 4–9

Location: full sun, fertile well-drained soil

Growing tip: Early spring is a favorite time to plant purple coneflowers. For the best success, select healthy, growing transplants not yet in bud.

Season of performance: summer through early autumn

Most gardeners don't realize the botanical name *Echinacea* means hedgehog. Name a prized variety 'Kim's Mophead' and the fun really starts. This garden featuring 'Kim's Mophead' and 'Kim's Knee High' purple coneflowers and 'Little Boy Phlox' packs beauty and fragrance on compact manageable plants. It also is a delight to wildlife, providing nectar for both butterflies and hummingbirds. Birds are also known to devour the seeds of the coneflowers.

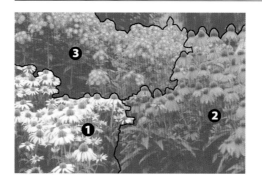

Old South Cottage Garden

Cottage gardens get their style from architecturally tall plants, and the old-fashioned hollyhock is certainly one that reaches for the sky. Most hollyhocks are considered short-lived perennials, but they're known to reseed, ensuring you'll have them for years to come. The annual larkspur and biennial Queen Anne's lace reseed as well. The yellow daylilies help create a triadic harmony with the hollyhocks and larkspurs. This garden was established several years prior to the photo being taken, but the original soil preparation was good and the plants were allowed to mature and self-sow.

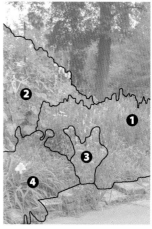

1 Larkspur (*Consolida ajacis*), annual

2 Hollyhock (*Alcea rosea*), zones 2–10

3 Queen Anne's lace (*Daucus carota*), biennial in zones 3–9

4 Daylily (*Hemerocallis* cv.), zones 3–10

Location: full to part sun, fertile well-drained soil

Growing tip: August and September are good months to plant hollyhocks and larkspurs from seed.

Season of performance: late spring and summer

A Passion for Poppies

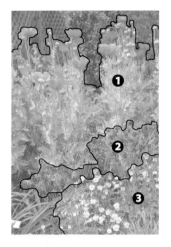

Lattice fences enhance the cottage style garden, especially when they serve as the backdrop for a stand of tall red poppies. These are the bread-seed or opium poppies that have reached heirloom status not only in European gardens but in the United States as well. The flowers can be cut for the vase, and the unique seedpods are useful in dried arrangements. Partner poppies with columbine and the award-winning 'Ultima Morpho' pansy, and you have a late spring combination that's hard to beat.

1 Poppy (*Papaver somniferum*), annual

2 European columbine (*Aquilegia vulgaris*), zones 3–8

3 'Ultima Morpho' pansy (*Viola* xwittrockiana 'Ultima Morpho'), annual

Location: full to part sun, well-drained soil

Growing tip: Let the poppies reseed and move seedlings as needed to desired location. Keep the seedlings moist, as they go through transplant shock.

Season of performance: late spring to summer

Shady Acres

Most think of the cottage garden as needing full sun, but some are sun challenged, to say the least. If you have part shade or an area of your garden a little on the shady side, you can't beat this partnership of the Chinese foxglove and strawberry geranium. Even in mid to late summer after the strawberry geranium has bloomed, the evergreen foliage is striking and certainly complements the Chinese foxglove. The pink tubular blossoms of the foxglove are reminiscent of the digitalis foxglove but larger and equally stunning, and they repeat bloom.

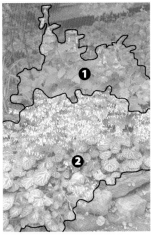

1 Chinese foxglove (*Rehmannia elata*), zones 7–11

2 Strawberry geranium (*Saxifraga stolonifera*), zones 6–9

Location: part sun, fertile well-drained soil

Growing tip: The foxglove should be deadheaded for return blooms. Both plants can spread, so manage your plots accordingly.

Season of performance: summer and autumn

Sizzling Summer Cottage

Despite its location in a climate of sweltering heat and humidity, this color ful garden stops traffic all summer as passersby gaze at the splendor. Here easy-to-grow foliage plays a vital role. The chartreuse 'Sweet Caroline Light Green' sweet potatoes look lush and tropical, complementing everything around them, like the 'Rustic Orange' coleus and succulent looking 'Purple Heart'. 'Bengal Tiger' canna in the background harmonizes with both its lime green variegated foliage and orange blossoms. The garden also fea tures an abundance of typical cottage flowers, such as salvias, black-eyed Susans, and zinnias.

1 'Tonto' crape myrtle (*Lagerstroemia xfauriei* 'Tonto'), zones 7–10

2 'Bengal Tiger' canna (*Canna xgeneralis* 'Bengal Tiger'), zones 7–10

3 'Sweet Caroline Light Green' sweet potato (*Ipomoea batatas* 'Sweet Caroline Light Green'), annual

4 'Rustic Orange' coleus (*Solenostemon scutellarioides* 'Rustic Orange'), annual

5 Dusty miller (*Senecio cineraria*), annual, perennial in zones 7–10

6 'Purple Heart' setcreasea (*Tradescantia pallida* 'Purple Heart'), zones 7–10

7 'Lady in Red' salvia (*Salvia coccinea* 'Lady in Red'), reseeding annual, perennial in zones 9–10

8 'Victoria Blue' mealy-cup sage (*Salvia farinacea* 'Victoria Blue'), annual, perennial in zones 7–10

9 Morning glory (*Ipomoea purpurea* cv.), annual, perennial in zones 9–11

10 Purslane mix (*Purslane grandiflora* cv.), annual

11 'Swizzle Cherry and Ivory' zinnia (*Zinnia violacea* 'Swizzle Cherry and Ivory'), annual

12 'Million Gold' melampodium (*Melampodium divaricatum* 'Million Gold'), annual

Location: full to part sun, moist fertile well-drained soil

Growing tip: Evergreen foundation plants are often overlooked but are essential for most gardens.

Season of performance: late spring through early autumn

Strolling to Margaritaville

This garden is thriving in a fertile organic-rich bed comprised of composted cotton burrs. Large drifts of perennials in pink, purple, red, and gray combined with tall blue reseeding larkspurs, cherry pink petunias, and strategically placed yellow from sedum and daylilies lead you to a shady retreat called Margaritaville.

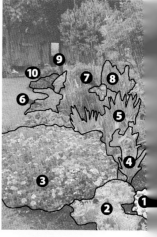

1 Petunia (*Petunia* cv.**),** annual

2 Gold moss sedum (*Sedum acre*), zones 3–8

3 Verbena (*Verbena canadensis* cv.), annual, perennial in zones 6–10

4 Amaryllis (*Hippeastrum* cv.), zones 8–10

5 Iris (*Iris* cv.), zones 3–10

6 'Purple Wave' petunia (*Petunia* 'Purple Wave'), annual

7 'Stella d'Oro' daylily (*Hemerocallis* 'Stella d'Oro'), zones 3–9

8 Larkspur (*Consolida ajacis*), annual

9 'Powis Castle' artemisia (*Artemisia* 'Powis Castle'), zones 5–8

10 'Purple Heart' setcreasea (*Tradescantia pallida* 'Purple Heart'), zones 7–10

Location: full sun, well-drained soil rich with organic matter

Growing tip: Group plants in informal drifts of single colors, rather than spot planting.

Season of performance: late spring through autumn

Violet Voyage

'All Around Purple' gomphrena, native to Panama and Guatemala, is a very easy plant to grow. If you don't recognize the name gomphrena, these plants are also known as globe amaranth and bachelor's button. Gomphrenas are incredibly tough and yet beautiful plants in the summer flower border or cottage garden. Its complementing partner here is the 'Profusion Deep Apricot' zinnia, another stalwart performer. With its vigor and disease resistance, the Profusion series has put the fun back into growing zinnias.

1 'All Around Purple' gomphrena (*Gomphrena globosa* 'All Around Purple'), annual

2 'Profusion Deep Apricot' zinnia (*Zinnia* 'Profusion Deep Apricot'), annual

Location: full sun, fertile well-drained soil

Growing tip: The gomphrena is an excellent cut flower as well as dried and used for winter arrangements. The little ball-shaped flowers also are ideal for adding to potpourri dishes.

Season of performance: spring through autumn

Containers

About half of American households do some form of container gardening. It's easier to provide a good environment for your plants when it comes to soil or potting mixes versus fighting poor conditions in the landscape. Containers are easier to maintain from the standpoint of water, fertilizer and competing weeds. Root-borne diseases are practically nonexistent. If containers are watered frequently, however, the nutrients quickly leach, meaning you need to fertilize more often.

Another advantage of containers is that they are movable. We can simply place them in the sunlight conditions that are best for the particular grouping of plants. Everyone in the country could be a citrus grower by growing the plants in a container and moving it to a protected place during the winter. Containers can also enhance the look of a patio or be used to decorate other parts of your property where plants can't be placed in the ground.

For each of the combinations in this section, I suggest using lightweight potting mix. Other than making sure the container has holes for water drainage, this is the most important criteria. It seems wherever you look there are ads promoting a $1.49 special for a 40-pound bag of potting soil, but these bags feel like they weigh about 60 pounds. Truthfully this heavy product seldom yields healthy container-grown plants. It's prone to holding water that will inevitably prove fatal to your flowers. The containers will be harder to move, and it will take more bags to get pots filled. Good lightweight potting soils are usually not sold by the pound but by the cubic foot. Though the bags are twice as large as the $1.49 special, they are easy to pick up and load. Many have controlled release fertilizer mixed in. Though these bags are more expensive, you'll need fewer of them, the planted containers will be easier to move, and the plants will thrive.

The recipe for designing a container for beauty and interest has three components: thriller, spiller, and filler. The thriller plant is usually the tall-

est and planted in the middle, reaching out and grabbing your interest by its texture or incredible beauty. Spiller plants fall over the edge and may even reach the ground. The filler plants may be greenery, colorful foliage, or flowers, and these are placed in the pockets in between the thriller and spiller plants. Container gardening allows you to be the Monet of your project. Have fun.

African Thriller

Containers need not have a lot of different plants to be captivating, especially when one of the plants is the floriferous 'Tidal Wave Hot Pink' petunia. The 'Maurelii' banana from Africa is well over 6 feet tall and lush, bringing a touch of the tropics to this deck and thrilling in every aspect. Its rich burgundy shades combine with the hot pink petunias for a harmonious marriage. The 'Suncatcher Sapphire' petunias have strong hints of red in the rare blue flowers and are simply marvelous in this colorful partnership.

1 'Maurelii' red Abyssinian banana (*Ensete ventricosum* 'Maurelii'), annual, perennial in zones 9–11

2 'Tidal Wave Hot Pink' petunia (*Petunia* 'Tidal Wave Hot Pink'), annual

3 'Suncatcher Sapphire' petunia (*Petunia* 'Suncatcher Sapphire'), annual

Location: full sun, lightweight potting soil

Growing tip: Keep the plants watered and fed, and cut back petunias to generate new growth and blooms.

Season of performance: summer through autumn

Butterfly Bowl

Butterflies will love this garden in a bowl. The tall 'Pink Delight' buddleia attracts butterflies and thrills the senses with fragrance. The 6- to 9-inch-wide flowers of 'Indian Summer' make it the container's thriller, while 'New Gold' lantana is a known butterfly magnet and serves as a bright and cheerful filler. The unbelievable spiller, 'Million Bells Cherry Pink' calibrachoa with scores of tubular flowers, will entice frequent visits by hummingbirds.

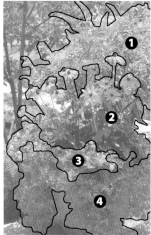

1 'Pink Delight' buddleia (*Buddleja davidii* 'Pink Delight'), zones 5–9

2 'Indian Summer' black-eyed Susan (*Rudbeckia hirta* 'Indian Summer'), zones 3–8

3 'New Gold' lantana (*Lantana* 'New Gold'), zones (7) 8–10

4 'Million Bells Cherry Pink' calibrachoa (*Calibrachoa* 'Million Bells Cherry Pink'), annual, perennial in zones 9–10

Location: full sun, lightweight potting soil

Growing tip: Deadheading and cutting back is crucial to reblooming in this container.

Season of performance: summer through autumn

Chaotic Blast of Pink

Place tropical hot pink on the porch, patio, or deck, and you'll have a re sort-like atmosphere ready for fun and partying. The theme begins wit the tall 'Spirit Violeta' cleome as the thriller plant in the center. Next is layer of 'Pink Chaos' coleus that matches in a wild monochromatic blen and reaches 12 to 18 inches tall with an equal spread. Finally, the vigorou 'Supertunia Raspberry Blast' petunia gently cascades over the edge. Thi container will be a hit with visitors to your home as well as butterflies an hummingbirds.

1 'Spirit Violeta' cleome (*Cleome hassleriana* 'Spirit Violeta'), annual

2 'Supertunia Raspberry Blast' petunia (*Petunia* 'Supertunia Raspberry Blast'), annual

3 'Pink Chaos' coleus (*Solenostemon scutellarioides* 'Pink Chaos'), annual

Location: full to part sun, lightweight potting soil

Growing tip: Keep plants fed with dilute water-soluble fertilizer.

Season of performance: summer through autumn

Cobalt Blue

The unbelievable iridescent cobalt blue of the 'Senetti Blue' draws attention like few other plants. Even though this selection doesn't bloom all summer, you'll still be mesmerized by its beauty. In frost-free areas, the plants will bloom from January through June. The blue of 'Senetti Blue' has red hues and thus a strong partner for the flamboyant foliage of the 'Bloodleaf' iresine. The hint of yellow in the photo is from an old leaf of the container's thriller plant, the 'Maurelii' red Abyssinian banana. The iresine and the banana will perform until freezing temperatures arrive.

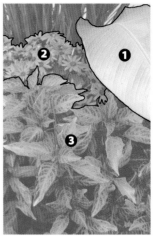

1 'Maurelii' red Abyssinian banana (*Ensete ventricosum* 'Maurelii'), zones 9–11

2 'Senetti Blue' cineraria (*Pericallis* 'Senetti Blue'), annual, perennial in zones 9–11

3 'Bloodleaf' iresine (*Iresine herbstii* 'Bloodleaf'), annual

Location: full to part sun, lightweight potting soil

Growing tip: After blooming, cut the 'Senetti Blue' back to generate growth and rebloom.

Season of performance: spring through autumn

Emeralds and Sapphires

Lime green is a hot color in the garden, and the 'Limón' talinum provides this jewel of a color. With its emerald color shining radiantly you have to agree it's a perfect complement for the sapphire-colored 'Easy Wave Blue' petunia. 'Easy Wave Blue' is a vigorous spreading petunia with a slightly mounding habit. 'Limón', a native of the West Indies and Central America, is commonly called jewels of Opar. The succulent-looking foliage quickly sends up arching panicles of hot pink star-shaped flowers.

1 'Limón' talinum (*Talinum paniculatum* 'Limón'), annual, perennial in zones (8) 9–11

2 'Easy Wave Blue' petunia (*Petunia* 'Easy Wave Blue'), annual

Location: full to part sun, lightweight potting soil

Growing tip: The long panicles of flowers and fruit capsules of 'Limón' are perfect for cutting and using like you would baby's breath.

Season of performance: spring and summer

Four-Part Harmony

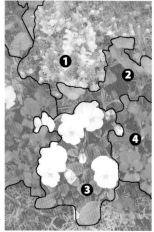

Like a four-part musical harmony, this cool-season planter uses color harmony to perfection. This planter is cold hardy, colorful, and fragrant. 'Fantasy Blue' linaria resembles a miniature snapdragon and is used similarly and planted in the same season (autumn in the South or early spring in the North). 'Polar Purple' dianthus, a selection new to most gardeners, offers deeply saturated colors, fragrance, and early blooming. 'Nature Yellow' pansies are some of the more weather tough available for the landscape. The 'Nature Yellow' seems to glow adjacent to the complementing 'Gem Sapphire' violas.

1 'Fantasy Blue' linaria
(*Linaria maroccana* 'Fantasy Blue'), annual

2 'Polar Purple' dianthus
(*Dianthus barbatus* x *chinensis* 'Polar Purple'), zones 4–9

3 'Nature Yellow' pansy
(*Viola* x*wittrockiana* 'Nature Yellow'), annual

4 'Gem Sapphire' viola
(*Viola cornuta* 'Gem Sapphire'), annual

Location: full sun, light-weight potting soil

Growing tip: This planter is a basket lined with sphagnum moss and filled with soil.

Season of performance: autumn through spring in the South, spring through early summer in the North

Kings and Angels

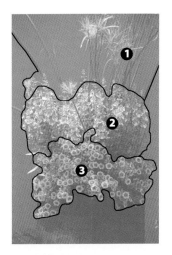

Regardless of whether you have a colorfully painted home, this container will add pizzazz all growing season. The tall and graceful 'King Tut' papyru lends a grass-like texture and commands attention. The rare blue come from 'ANGELFACE Wedgwood Blue' angelonia or summer snapdragon, a plant that is ruggedly durable in landscapes or containers. The blue is a remarkable complementary color for the 'Superbells Apricot Punch' cali brachoa, whose tubular flowers bring visits from darting hummingbirds.

1 'King Tut' papyrus (*Cyperus papyrus* 'King Tut'), annual, perennial in zones 8–11

2 'ANGELFACE Wedgwood Blue' angelonia (*Angelonia angustifolia* 'ANGELFACE Wedgwood Blue'), annual, perennial in zones 9–11

3 'Superbells Apricot Punch' calibrachoa (*Calibrachoa* 'Superbells Apricot Punch'), annual, perennial in zones (8) 9–11

Location: full to part sun, lightweight potting soil

Growing tip: Summer containers that get watered everyday need regular feeding, as nutrients are rapidly leached.

Season of performance: summer through early autumn

Magical Falls

This waterfall was already spectacular, but a well-placed container with a monochromatic blend of blues and violets turned it into a real garden. The blue color scheme is a natural accompaniment to flowing water. The angelonias take center stage by virtue of being tall and spiky. The silver light lavender of the 'Aztec Silver Magic' verbena echoes the intense blue of the petunia. The 'Angel Mist Pink' angelonias that are planted in the distance create additional excitement and give continuity in texture.

1 'Angel Mist Purple Stripe' angelonia (*Angelonia angustifolia* 'Angel Mist Purple Stripe'), annual, perennial in zones 9–11

2 'Wave Blue' petunia (*Petunia* 'Wave Blue'), annual

3 'Aztec Silver Magic' verbena (*Verbena* 'Aztec Silver Magic'), annual, perennial in zones 6–10

4 'Angel Mist Pink' angelonia (*Angelonia angustifolia* 'Angel Mist Pink'), annual, perennial in zones 9–11

Location: full sun, lightweight potting soil

Growing tip: Shallow containers need close monitoring as they dry much more quickly.

Season of performance: summer through autumn

Photo courtesy of Terry Howe, Ball Horticultural Co.

Melody in Bloom

Everyone would cherish this mixed container that harmonizes the color so brilliantly and yet gives months of outstanding performance. 'Gage's Shadow', which resembles a coleus, brings colorful foliage that blends with both the leaves and flowers of the 'ANGELFACE Dark Violet' angelonia. Also called summer snapdragon, the angelonia gives the container a spiky feature that contrasts with its round-flowered companions, the petunia, scarlet calibrachoa, and yellow chrysocephalum. Native to the West Indies, angelonia is able to tolerate high heat and humidity.

1 'Gage's Shadow' perilla (*Perilla frutescens* 'Gage's Shadow'), annual, perennial in zones 10–11

2 'ANGELFACE Dark Violet' angelonia (*Angelonia angustifolia* 'ANGELFACE Dark Violet'), annual, perennial in zones 9–11

3 'Flambe Yellow' chrysocephalum (*Chrysocephalum apiculatum* 'Flambe Yellow'), annual, perennial in zones 7–10

4 'Supertunia Royal Velvet' petunia (*Petunia* 'Supertunia Royal Velvet'), annual

5 'Superbells Scarlet' calibrachoa (*Calibrachoa* 'Superbells Scarlet'), annual, perennial in zones (8) 9–11

Location: full sun, lightweight potting soil

Growing tip: Watering everyday in the summer leaches nutrients so feed regularly.

Season of performance: summer through autumn

An Old Masterpiece

The weathered old container makes this combination a picturesque piece of art one might find at a historic inn. The 'Etain' viola is a fragrant delight that's easy to grow. Its lavender edges contrast with the golden blades of the fine-textured leaves of sweet flag. Even finer in texture and equally the complement is the 'Lemon Coral' sedum, with needle-shaped leaves. Though tiny, 'Thumbell' bellflowers lend added visual interest.

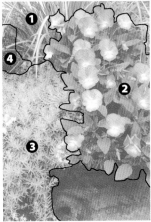

1 'Ogon' golden variegated sweet flag (*Acorus gramineus* 'Ogon'), zones 5–11

2 'Etain' viola (*Viola* hybrid 'Etain'), annual, perennial in zones 3–8

3 'Lemon Coral' sedum (*Sedum rupestre* 'Lemon Coral'), zones 3–11

4 'Thumbell' bellflower (*Campanula rotundifolia* 'Thumbell'), zones 3–8

Location: part shade, lightweight potting soil

Growing tip: There is nothing wrong with treating some or all of the plants as annuals to keep this combination always at its showiest. Replace some as hot weather arrives, so that the planter always remains at its best.

Season of performance: autumn through spring in the South, spring and summer in the North

Painted Patio

A couple of large mixed containers on a small patio can give a season of floral bliss. Combining foliage and flowers that drape to the ground and hide the pots creates a sense of mystery and excitement about the structure of the containers. The various blue shades of 'Patina Purple', 'Arcade Trailing Blue', and 'Sanguna Atomic Blue' show a little hint of pink and boldly contrast with both the silver leaves of 'Beacon Silver' lamium and the emerging lime of 'Goldii' lysimachia.

1 'Beacon Silver' lamium (*Lamium maculatum* 'Beacon Silver'), zones 3–9

2 'Patina Purple' ageratum (*Ageratum houstonianum* 'Patina Purple'), annual

3 'Arcade Trailing Blue' lobelia (*Lobelia erinus* 'Arcade Trailing Blue'), annual

4 'Magelana Salmon Rose' verbena (*Verbena* 'Magelana Salmon Rose'), annual, perennial in zones 6–10

5 'Goldii' lysimachia (*Lysimachia nummularia* 'Goldii'), zones 3–11

6 'Sanguna Atomic Blue' petunia (*Petunia* 'Sanguna Atomic Blue'), annual

Location: full to part sun, lightweight potting soil

Growing tip: Cutting back plants in late summer will generate growth and blooms for autumn.

Season of performance: summer through autumn

Paradise with Paprika

'Oso Easy Paprika' rose echoes the rich colors found in the leaves of 'Beyond Paradise' copper plant. In a bright sunny garden the colors are even more stunning. 'Oso Easy Paprika' is compact, reaching only 2 feet tall. The dark violet of the angelonia and the petunia complement the orange and cream colors. 'Beyond Paradise' lends a touch of the tropics to gardens and is well suited to being the thriller plant in large mixed containers.

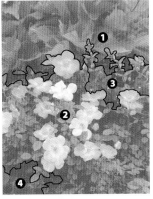

1 'Beyond Paradise' copper plant (*Acalypha wilkesiana* 'Beyond Paradise'), annual, perennial in zones 9–11

2 'Oso Easy Paprika' rose (*Rosa* 'Oso Easy Paprika'), zones 5–9

3 'ANGELFACE Dark Violet' angelonia (*Angelonia angustifolia* 'ANGELFACE Dark Violet'), annual, perennial in zones 9–11

4 'Supertunia Royal Velvet' petunia (*Petunia* 'Supertunia Royal Velvet'), annual

Location: full sun, lightweight potting soil

Growing tip: Feed this combination every 4 to 6 weeks. Deadhead roses and angelonia as needed.

Season of performance: late spring through autumn

Perfume Delight

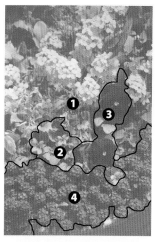

Container gardening is for cool months, too. As this container demonstrates, cool-season combinations can be colorful and tantalizing with fragrance. Each plant in the container is a small perfume factory. The tall 'Citrona Orange' erysimum, a member of the cabbage family, provides a fiery contrast with the purple from the pansies and alyssum. 'Sorbet Sunny Royale' viola is wonderful in that it either harmonizes or contrasts with every other plant in the container. 'Easter Bonnet Violet' alyssum softly tumbles over the rim of the container.

1 'Citrona Orange' erysimum (*Erysimum* 'Citrona Orange'), annual

2 'Sorbet Sunny Royale' viola (*Viola cornuta* 'Sorbet Sunny Royale'), annual

3 'Matrix Purple' pansy (*Viola xwittrockiana* 'Matrix Purple'), annual

4 'Easter Bonnet Violet' alyssum (*Lobularia maritima* 'Easter Bonnet Violet'), annual

Location: full to part sun, lightweight potting soil

Growing tip: Feed with dilute water-soluble fertilizer every other week.

Season of performance: autumn through spring in the South, spring through early summer in the North

Pineapple and Paradise

'Pineapple Splash' is the focal point of this container, with its uniquely shaped poinsettia-like foliage featuring bright yellow and crimson. The crimson veins echo the color of the 'Tukana Scarlet' verbena, which gently cascades over the rim. The tropical 'Beyond Paradise' copper plant and 'Dolce Peach Melba' heuchera lend their own blends of red, tying everything together in one terrific display.

1 'Beyond Paradise' copper plant (*Acalypha wilkesiana* 'Beyond Paradise'), annual, perennial in zones 9–11

2 'Pineapple Splash' coleus (*Solenostemon scutellarioides* 'Pineapple Splash'), annual

3 'Tukana Scarlet' verbena (*Verbena* hybrid 'Tukana Scarlet'), annual, perennial in zone 7–11

4 'Dolce Peach Melba' heuchera (*Heuchera* 'Dolce Peach Melba'), zones 5–11

Location: full to part sun, lightweight potting soil

Growing tip: Cut back verbena periodically to generate new growth and blooms. Pinch coleus as needed to keep bushy.

Season of performance: summer through autumn

Shining Lanterns

The 'Golden Lanterns' variety of Himalayan honeysuckle represents every thing you might want in a thriller plant in a mixed container. If the plan never bloomed you would still love it, but it does bear white flowers and purple bracts that give way to purple berries in autumn. 'Toffee Twist sedge has a bronze grassy texture. 'Supertunia Royal Velvet' falls over the edge of the container and is an ideal foil for the psychedelic lime green leaves of 'Golden Lantern'.

1 'Golden Lanterns' Himalayan honeysuckle (*Leycesteria formosa* 'Golden Lanterns'), annual, perennial in zones 6b–9

2 'Supertunia Royal Velvet' petunia (*Petunia* 'Supertunia Royal Velvet'), annual

3 'Toffee Twist' sedge (*Carex flagellifera* 'Toffee Twist'), annual, perennial in zones 7–11

Location: full to part sun, lightweight potting soil

Growing tip: The 'Supertunia Royal Velvet' responds well to cutting back in late summer.

Season of performance: summer through autumn

Tropical Treasure

The elegant and welcoming areca palm allows everyone to have a taste of the tropics. Because the frost-free season in the United States is long, the areca is a great value for your budget and a wonderful attention-grabbing thriller plant. The 'Titan Lilac' vinca serves as a colorful floral transition to the explosive golden lime of the duranta, which gently spills over the rim of the container.

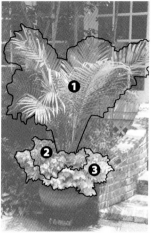

1 Areca palm (*Chrysalidocarpus lutescens*), zones 10–11

2 'Titan Lilac' vinca (*Catharanthus roseus* 'Titan Lilac'), annual

3 'Gold Mound' duranta (*Duranta erecta* 'Gold Mound'), annual zones 8–11

Location: full to part sun, lightweight potting mix

Growing tip: Feed with a dilute water-soluble fertilizer every other week. The areca palm is well suited to overwintering in brightly lit areas indoors.

Season of performance: late spring through autumn

Tumbling Waterfall

'Waterfall Blue' lobelia is one of the most intensely blue flowers available for the garden and is perfect for creating the impression of flowing water. 'Waterfall Blue' will be simply unbeatable during the spring but diminishing once the intense heat of summer begins. In cooler areas, it will bloom all summer. The complementing partner is 'Riverdene Gold' Mexican heather, whose lime green leaves echo the leaf margins of the blazing 'Rustic Orange' coleus.

1 'Waterfall Blue' lobelia (*Lobelia erinus* 'Waterfall Blue'), annual

2 'Riverdene Gold' Mexican heather (*Cuphea hyssopifolia* 'Riverdene Gold'), annual, perennial in zones (8) 9–11

3 'Rustic Orange' coleus (*Solenostemon scutellarioides* 'Rustic Orange'), annual

Location: full sun, lightweight potting soil

Growing tip: Keep 'Rustic Orange' bushy and vibrantly colored by pinching throughout the summer.

Season of performance: spring through summer

Patriotic

In World War II, victory gardens helped meet the needs of rationed goods. Today, many Americans want to express pride in our country, much like our parents and grandparents did with their victory gardens. Hence we are seeing a steady increase in gardens that bring together the colors red, white, and blue. A patriotic summer display is easy to develop either in the garden or a container.

New choices of angelonias, petunias, salvias, and verbenas make it easy and fun. Consider a combination planting with 'Fantasia Strawberry Sizzle' geranium with 'Cloud Nine White' and 'Cloud Nine Blue' ageratums. Petunias like 'Easy Wave Red', 'Easy Wave Blue', 'Storm Blue' and 'Storm Red' can be combined with white flowers like 'Diamond Frost' euphorbia, 'Abunda Giant White' bacopa, and 'Spirit Frost' cleome. Look also for perennial verbenas in these patriotic colors. The Tukana, Aztec, and Tapien series offer some of the richest colors coupled with superior flower power. Don't forget spiky flowers like 'Mystic Spires Blue', 'Black and Blue', and 'Victoria Blue' salvias and the incredible 'ANGELFACE Wedgwood Blue' angelonia.

Another option would be to include a gazing globe in the place of a particular color of flower, such as a blue gazing globe with red salvias and white verbenas or some combination that appeals to you. The gazing globe was a symbol during the Depression that we would come out of the financial crisis. Having a beautiful summer landscape filled with red, white, and blue will make a statement of your faith in the country's future and that God will bless America.

Blissfully Patriotic

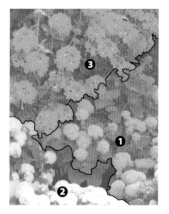

If you are on Cloud Nine you are ecstatic or blissfully happy. This may ver[y] well be how you feel once you start growing this series of ageratums o[f] the same name. The large clusters of showy flowers attract butterflie[s] and hummingbirds and butterflies will also be congregating on the 'Azte[c] Cherry Red' verbenas. Aztec series verbenas are not prone to powdery mil[-] dew and reach around 10 inches tall and 2 to 3 feet wide.

1 'Cloud Nine Blue' ageratum (*Ageratum houstonianum* 'Cloud Nine Blue'), annual

2 'Cloud Nine White' ageratum (*Ageratum houstonianum* 'Cloud Nine White'), annual

3 'Aztec Cherry Red' verbena (*Verbena* 'Aztec Cherry Red'), annual, perennial in zones 6–10

Location: full sun, fertile well-drained soil

Growing tip: Feed every 4 to 6 weeks with controlled release granules or every 2 to 3 weeks with dilute water-soluble fertilizer.

Season of performance: summer through autumn

Blutopian Vista

Deep rose and light blue make an enticing combination. The Vista series has become one of the most popular series of scarlet sage, staying compact and showing excellent heat tolerance. Much to the delight of hummingbirds, they perform all summer long. Here the partner is the first seed-produced bacopa selection. 'Blutopia' is a trailing or spreading plant, making it an excellent choice for a planter box such as the one pictured. It blooms heaviest in the spring and autumn.

1 'Vista Rose' scarlet sage
(*Salvia splendens* 'Vista Rose'), annual

2 'Blutopia' bacopa
(*Sutera cordata* 'Blutopia'), annual

Location: full to part sun, lightweight potting soil

Growing tip: Cut back 'Blutopia' in midsummer to encourage branching. In the Deep South, locate containers in morning sun and filtered afternoon light.

Season of performance: spring and autumn

1 'Cloud Nine Blue' and 'Cloud Nine White' ageratum (*Ageratum houstonianum* 'Cloud Nine Blue' and 'Cloud Nine White'), annual

2 'Fantasia Strawberry Sizzle' and 'Fantasia Cardinal Red' geranium (*Pelargonium xhortorum* 'Fantasia Strawberry Sizzle' and 'Fantasia Cardinal Red'), annual

Location: full to part sun, a little afternoon shade in the hot South, fertile well-drained soil rich with organic matter

Growing tip: Prompt removal of the spent geranium flower stalks improves performance. Cut back stems to promote bushiness.

Season of performance: summer through autumn

Clouds of Fantasy

This stunning display would make a bold statement in any garden. The Cloud Nine series isn't your grandmother's ageratum. These ageratums made a stunning debut with their habit and large blooms. Partner both colors with the dark-green-leafed Fantasia geraniums, and you'll find yourself flag waving, too. The Fantasia series of geraniums, with large semi-double blossoms, offer great heat tolerance as well.

The Devil and the Lady

The mention of 'Rozanne' snuggling up to 'Lucifer' sounds like a young lady gone to the dark side, but in the garden it's a partnership you would be proud to show the preacher. 'Lucifer', the most sought after of all crocosmias (or monbretias), produces large sword-shaped foliage that reaches 3 to 4 feet long and produces fiery red blooms that face upward on branched spikes. This gladiola relative makes a bold statement when partnered with the violet blue flowers of 'Rozanne', an award-winning perennial cranesbill geranium.

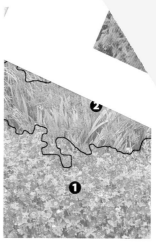

1 'Rozanne' geranium (*Geranium* 'Rozanne'), zones 5–8

2 'Lucifer' crocosmia (*Crocosmia* 'Lucifer'), zones 5–9

Location: full to part sun, afternoon shade protection in the South, well-drained soil

Growing tip: If 'Rozanne' gets leggy or thin, cut plants to 3 inches, which will stimulate growth, bushiness, and bloom.

Season of performance: summer

Photo courtesy of Blooms of Bressingham

How Sweet It Is

Patriotic colors aren't just for the summer—this display will thrive during cooler months. The Sweet series of dianthus, reminiscent of the old sweet William, is a good cut flower and terrific landscape performer and offers delightful fragrance and beauty. Coral is a nice addition to the patriotic garden. The 'Sorbet Blue Babyface' viola is unique in two ways: it is blue and has a blotch that is more typical of pansies.

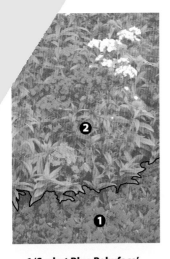

1 'Sorbet Blue Babyface' viola (*Viola cornuta* 'Sorbet Blue Babyface'), annual

2 'Sweet White', 'Sweet Scarlet', 'Sweet Coral' dianthus (*Dianthus barbatus* Sweet series), annual, perennial in zones 3–7 (8)

Location: full to part sun, fertile well-drained soil rich with organic matter

Growing tip: Prompt deadheading of spent flowers increases the chances of dianthus becoming a perennial.

Season of performance: autumn through spring in the South, spring through summer in the North

Hurrah for the USA

Many gardeners aren't familiar with laurentia, but when they see these rare soft blue star-shaped flowers they'll give these plants a try. Though the flowers are small, the color of this native Australian stands out in contrast to the pristine white petunia and red verbena. The differing flower sizes and shapes create visual interest. While this planting works in the landscape, this colorful display is grown in a midsized container that would be easy for any gardener to duplicate for those Fourth of July parties.

1 'Hurrah White' petunia (*Petunia* 'Hurrah White'), annual

2 'Obsession Red with Eye' verbena (*Verbena* 'Obsession Red with Eye'), annual

3 'Starshine' laurentia (*Isotoma axillaris* 'Starshine'), annual, perennial in zones 10–11

Location: full sun, fertile well-drained soil

Growing tip: This verbena doesn't spread as much as other verbena selections and is perfect for filler type plantings.

Season of performance: early summer through autumn

Party On

This clustering of pots for a patriotic party of sorts shows what can be done on a moment's notice to show your colors. You can plant them in a large container, where the 'Mystic Spires Blue' is the thriller, 'Aztec Cherry Red' verbena is the filler, and the 'Abunda Giant White' bacopa will cascade over the rim as a spiller. They perform exceedingly well in the landscape. The 'Mystic Spires Blue' is the first compact selection from 'Indigo Spires' and gives a needed spiky texture to the garden.

1 'Mystic Spires Blue' salvia (*Salvia* 'Mystic Spires Blue'), annual, perennial in zones 7–11

2 'Abunda Giant White' bacopa (*Sutera cordata* 'Abunda Giant White'), annual

3 'Aztec Cherry Red' verbena (*Verbena* 'Aztec Cherry Red'), annual, perennial in zones 6–10

Location: full sun, fertile well-drained soil

Growing tip: Cut back each plant to encourage more branching and blooming.

Season of performance: summer through autumn

Patriotic Sages

This unique combination of red and blue salvias may have you singing "It's a Grand Old Flag." Hummingbirds will love this combination as well. 'Paul' offers a rare bright red in comparison to the burgundy you usually see in a wine sage. As more gardeners are growing anise sage, 'Black and Blue', with its deep blue flowers and black calyx, has become a popular selection. This combination will show your patriotic colors most vibrantly.

1 'Paul' wine sage (*Salvia vanhouttei* 'Paul'), annual, perennial in zones 8–10

2 'Black and Blue' anise sage (*Salvia guaranitica* 'Black and Blue'), annual, perennial in zones 7–10

Location: morning sun with a little afternoon shade protection, fertile well-drained soil

Growing tip: Good winter drainage and mulch will help encourage a spring return of these sages.

Season of performance: summer through autumn

Showing Your Spirit

White spidery flowers, spikes of blue snapdragon-like blooms, and round scarlet red flowers make this garden one of excitement and extra interest. If that weren't enough, this combination also attracts hummingbirds and butterflies. The Spirit series of cleome is unique in that it is vegetatively propagated, and these plants are gaining recognition in trials everywhere. Angelonias, sometimes called summer snapdragons, are from Mexico and the West Indies and have great heat tolerance. Butterflies love 'Tukana Scarlet' verbena, a vigorous, mounding, and season-long performer.

1 'Spirit Frost' cleome (*Cleome hassleriana* 'Spirit Frost'), annual

2 'ANGELFACE Wedgwood Blue' angelonia (*Angelonia angustifolia* 'ANGELFACE Wedgwood Blue'), annual, perennial in zones 9–11

3 'Tukana Scarlet' verbena (*Verbena* 'Tukana Scarlet'), annual, perennial in zones 7–11

Location: full to part sun, fertile well-drained soil

Growing tip: Cut back the verbenas and the angelonias as needed to stimulate growth and blooms.

Season of performance: summer through autumn

Waving Your Colors

Patriotic color schemes need not be complicated, they can be quite easy. 'Easy Wave Blue' and 'Easy Wave Red' are two of the eight colors in the Easy Wave series and, yes, there is an 'Easy Wave White'. The Easy Wave cultivars are spreading and grow in mounds to 12 inches in height. 'Easy Wave Blue' is vigorous and dark blue, capable of spreading to 3 feet. 'Easy Wave Red' opens deep and darkly saturated in color, finishing a softer red. It spreads to 3 feet as well.

1 'Easy Wave Red' petunia (*Petunia* 'Easy Wave Red'), annual

2 'Easy Wave Blue' petunia (*Petunia* 'Easy Wave Blue'), annual

Location: full sun, fertile well-drained soil rich with organic matter

Growing tip: Feed with a dilute water-soluble fertilizer every 3 to 4 weeks or use controlled release granules.

Season of performance: summer through autumn

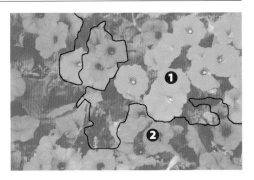

Bibliography

Armitage, Allan M. 2000. *Armitage's Garden Perennials: A Color Encyclopedia*. Portland, Ore.: Timber Press.

———. 2001. *Armitage's Manual of Annuals, Biennials, and Half-Hardy Perennials*. Portland, Ore.: Timber Press.

Bender, Steven, editor. 1998. *The Southern Living Garden Book*. Birmingham, Ala.: Oxmoor House.

Burrell, Colston C. 1999. *Perennial Combinations*. Emmaus, Penn.: Rodale Press.

Hill, Madalene, and Gwen Barclay, with Jean Hardy. 1987. *Southern Herb Growing*. Fredericksburg, Tex.: Shearer Publishing.

Hillier, Malcolm. 1995. *Malcolm Hillier's Color Garden*. New York: Dorling Kindersley.

Huxley, Anthony, editor. 1992. *The New Royal Horticultural Society Dictionary of Gardening*. New York: Stockton Press.

Lawson, Andrew. 1996. *The Gardener's Book of Color*. Pleasantville, N.Y.: The Readers Digest Association.

Welch, William C. 1989. *Perennial Garden Color*. Dallas, Tex.: Taylor Publishing.

Winter, Norman L. 2000. *Mississippi Gardener's Guide*. Franklin, Tenn.: Cool Springs Press.

———. 2001. *Paradise Found: Growing Tropicals in Your Own Backyard*. Dallas, Tex.: Taylor Publishing.

———. 2003. *Tough-as-Nails Flowers for the South*. Jackson, Miss.: University Press of Mississippi.

Index